THE RE
TEACHERS
GUIDEBOOK

THE REIKI TEACHERS GUIDEBOOK

A GUIDE FOR REIKI TEACHERS, PRACTITIONERS & STUDENTS

By Ricky Mathieson

WE ARE ONE
"To understand everything is to forgive everything." – **Buddha**

DISCLAIMER

This book offers non-specific, general advice and is not to be considered as a replacement for professional medical advice and consultation. Reiki helps to harmonize and balance the physical, mental, emotional and spiritual self and complements any medical treatments you may be receiving. It is advised that you consult a fully licensed medical professional should you have any acute or chronic medical conditions or diseases.

All information and treatments are offered in good faith and the author accepts no responsibility or liability for any loss or damage of any nature that may occur directly or indirectly as a result of relying upon the information contained herein or from the application or use of the information in this book, or from the failure to seek professional medical advice.

The moral right of the author has been asserted.

ISBN 978-1-326-06610-9

ACKNOWLEDGEMENTS

Many thanks to my teachers, my guides and all those who have directly or indirectly helped in the preparation and completion of this book.

To the Divine Source
For your continuous love, guidance and support.

Please note: Receiving training and attunements from a fully qualified Reiki Teacher is required before being able to perform the techniques listed in this book, which should not be considered as a substitute for that required initiation process.

For information about Reiki training or to contact the author please visit www.selfhelphealing.co.uk

ABOUT THE AUTHOR

❝ *The purpose of life is as much about transformation as it is about seeking new information. Information does not hold all the answers. The most important things in life can only be understood by the heart. Learn to open your heart and you will transform your world from the inside out.* ❞ - **Ricky Mathieson**

After an unintentional full activation of the Kundalini and subsequent spiritual awakening, Ricky has been guided towards opening himself further to the Divine gift of Spiritual Healing on his quest for absolute truth. A journey that has resulted in Ricky becoming a Reiki Master-Teacher in a number of healing modalities as well as becoming proficient in various additional pursuits including meditation, Neuro Linguistic Programming and Esotericism.

Ricky practices and teaches a combination of traditional Japanese Reiki, Tibetan Reiki and Indonesian Reiki and is an Usui Shiki Ryoho Master-Teacher, a Karuna Master-Teacher and a Reiki Tummo Master. Ricky has combined these disciplines with an avid interest and knowledge in psychology, metaphysics, natural phenomena and Mysticism and has dedicated his life to an on-going Yoga program in his quest towards enlightenment.

Ricky offers his students training and attunement in these Reiki disciplines and provides on-going assistance to individuals with their personal growth and spiritual development in mind. Ricky is also currently writing a unique self-help book, for the individual and humanity as a whole, which serves to revolutionize how we perceive the world while giving us a deeper understanding of our place in it. The book, *'Revolution X: Nefilibata'* is due to be published sometime in the year 2015.

INTRODUCTION

❝ Emotion is energy in motion & the energy of love within your heart connects you to the source of life. Where your attention goes your energy flows, so you are already an energy worker. You just may not be aware of it yet. ❞ - **Ricky Mathieson**

The human heart is the real key to accessing Divine guidance and for improving ones ability and potential to channel an ever increasing flow of Divine Reiki energy. Therefore working on connecting with the energy of our hearts should be one of the goals of every Reiki practitioner. Our heart has the ability to feel the things our eyes cannot see and knows what the mind can not understand. So when your head and heart conflicts, always follow your heart. Your heart already knows what you truly wish to become and it is through your heart that your connection to the Divine Source is realized. Your heart is the key to unlocking your full potential in this life and love is the key to its door.

Within the pages of this book you will find all the knowledge you need to become a powerful channel for the Divine energy of Reiki. Among many other things, you will discover the true history and origins of Reiki, how to use this energy in your every day life, what can be achieved with it and how to successfully set up your own Reiki business and spread this gift to the wider world. The preparation of the physical body and the mental and emotional bodies, as well as our connection to our spiritual selves, are all key elements that every Reiki Practitioner is encouraged to develop. The structure of this book has been styled to lay this foundation into your life.

Usui Reiki is not the answer. It is merely the first key to something far greater in nature. Use that key, open the door and discover who and what you really are. If you are not actively participating in the exchange of energies happening around and within you, you are subservient to them and at their mercy. Through taking the time to discover the deeper aspects of our inner selves, we will in time awaken to the truth about our Divine purpose and place in this world. Being a healer, Reiki Master or Spiritual Guru does not make you a special person. You are already a special person. If you do not yet see this, then your attention is too focused upon the outside world. You only have to take the time to attend to your inner self.

The true path to happiness and spiritual fulfillment lies dormant within each and every one of us and this is where you will find it, not in the outside world. When we live to serve our inner selves, we soon come to an understanding about one of lives absolute truths. That there is a sleeping power within each and every one of us that is infinitely more powerful than we have been led to believe. This power is not only a part of you. It is you. Reiki simply helps you discover and connect to your core power and will help bring about a new level of self-awareness.

The nature of Reiki offers us far more than the simple ability to heal. It gives us the tools and means to direct our lives for the highest and greatest good of all concerned. Take a moment to imagine a blank book and a magical pen that literally creates your future as you write it. It may sound like a wonderful fairy tale. In actual fact, this is one of the very gifts given to us through awakening to Reiki and our true nature.

Science has shown that everything in the Universe is energy which, at the atomic level, consists of different frequencies of vibrating particles. This includes your body, thoughts and emotions. Therefore one can correctly surmise that each of the events and situations you experience in your life can all be defined as different flows of energy. Everything you experience in the physical world is just a different flow of energy. Once you become aware of these energies and deepen your understanding of them, you can then use them to attract success, abundance, peace and happiness into your life.

By choosing your thoughts wisely and by carefully selecting which of your emotions you release and reinforce, you can determine the affects you will have upon the people around you and the wider world. It is these same thoughts and emotions that determine the nature of your lives experiences. You quite literally create and become what you think and everything that is in your life at the present moment is a direct result of what you have thought. Whether consciously or subconsciously. By opening yourself to Reiki and understanding how energy flows you can learn to direct it. Reiki helps stop our experiences from determining our existence and shows us how to use our existence to determine our experiences.

The journey into the world of Reiki is one filled with fascination, magic and love and Usui Reiki is the first key in showing us who and what we are and the healing potential we each hold. Whether you are interested in Reiki healing practices or are an experienced Master, I hope that the depth and heart of this book is found to be useful.

PART 1:

THE REIKI BASICS

All that we are is the result of what we have thought. The mind is everything. What we think we become. **– Buddha**

CHAPTER 1
DEDICATION TO DR. MIKAO USUI

&& *Every existence has healing power. Plants, trees, animals, fish and insects, but especially a human, as the lord of creation has remarkable power. Usui Reiki Ryoho is materialized as the healing power every human has.* && - **Mikao Usui**

Reiki founder, Mikao Usui, 15th Aug. 1865 – 9th Mar. 1926

This book wouldn't be complete without a loving dedication to the founder of Reiki, Dr. Mikao Usui, whose love, kindness and lifelong quest for spiritual understanding has helped enlighten the world and improved the lives of many. Through Dr. Usui's tireless efforts, he has inspired us with a new lease of belief for the future of humanity and the planet to which we belong. Master

Usui should be remembered for his contribution towards humanity.

As the initial wave of Reiki gathers pace, a new level of consciousness continues to awaken and enlighten the inhabitants of our planet. Many of us have already opened ourselves to the truth about the world we live in, the hidden world we rarely see and what we are truly capable of. Thanks to Dr. Usui and those he taught, humanity has taken a magnificent leap forward in spiritual evolution. What would usually take years of dedicated practise and meditation can now easily be achieved in a matter of days.

Mikao Usui was aware that every living thing, plants, trees, animals, fish, insects and humans, has an energy field that surrounds and interpenetrates it. Everything in the Universe is energy, including you, and whether aware of it or not, you are constantly interacting with the energy fields all around you. This is an important point to be aware of because your energy field directly affects your health and well-being. If your energy field is left persistently unbalanced, you will be more susceptible to ill health and disease. Using the power of Reiki, we are able to channel high frequency healing energy into our bodies and surrounding energy field to keep us in this state of well-being. The high frequency vibrations of Reiki break up and release the negative low vibrations from our body and being and when our energy field is healthy, so too is our body and mind.

CHAPTER 2
WHAT IS REIKI SHIKI RYOHO

❝ *Rule your mind or it will rule you.* ❞ - **Buddha**

Reiki Shiki Ryoho is a specific form of energy practice that opens a practitioners mind, body and consciousness in order to connect with the Universal energies of Reiki. This gives one the necessary tools and ability to positively affect their own self-growth and development and helps one become aware of their true spiritual selves. Reiki is translated to mean *'Spiritual Life Energy',* and its power is both unfathomable and immeasurable. Being the Universal Life Force, it is a power that's incomprehensible to man and womankind. This power can not be understood by intellect alone. It has to be experienced.

Reiki Shiki Ryoho is pronounced *'Ray-Key Shi-Key Ro-Ho'.* Reiki means *'Spiritual Life Energy'.* Shiki means *'System'* and Ryoho means *'Method of Healing'.* As Reiki has passed down the lineage from one master to the next, the practice has developed through the influences of social events, the personal experiences of the lineage bearer and the spiritual guidance of the Divine source of Reiki.

The core of the practice taught in Usui's healing system emphasizes the value and importance of self-treatment first and foremost and then the treatment of family and friends in order to become knowledgeable about the nature of Reiki as one continues to experience the gift of healing and personal growth. Reiki First Degree gives you the necessary foundation needed to grow and develop through this mysterious connection to Reiki, the Universal Life Force, and the influences of the unseen spiritual realm. The basic teachings of Reiki involve healing the self and others using the seven main Chakras and the various energy symbols that are gifted at each progressive level. Reiki is not a religion and it holds no dogmas, doctrines, creeds

5

or contradictions to the universal laws of consciousness and love. The energy itself helps one in developing unconditional love and compassion, both for oneself and all other life forms alike. It is not necessary to prepare oneself to receive a Reiki attunement, as no matter where each student may be at any point in their life, Reiki will intelligently harmonize each individual in such a way that is unique for their individual circumstances and needs. Provided you are willing, Reiki will bring its Divine presence to your life and awaken you to your true spiritual nature and Divine purpose in life. Your goal is to discover that purpose.

When you receive each Reiki attunement at the various levels, you will open a permanent channel to this spiritual life-force energy. This will begin an automatic journey towards self-realization and discovery without the need to consciously alter ones mind through meditation, prayer, or creative visualization. Reiki will awaken you to your path and lead you towards your unique life purpose and Divine destiny. We need only trust in it.

While visualizing the Reiki symbols during a treatment can help with ones understanding and relationship with these different energies, all that is necessary is to place your hands upon either yourself or another with the intention to channel this healing energy. This will automatically start the flow of Reiki. Reiki is the life force of all things, making it the very creative source of energy that many refer to as the God-Force and the power and possibilities that come with it are truly limitless.

Reiki is a form of holistic therapy, meaning it heals every aspect of an individual, mind, body and spirit. It can also be used as a complementary therapy with any other form of health care, as it helps to enhance the effectiveness of each one. It does not interfere with modern medicine in any way and helps to facilitate a deeper level of healing for those who practise and receive it. Reiki can help to alleviate pain and discomfort, speed up the body's natural healing process and can help to provide your body with the extra energy needed when one may be ill, receiving medical treatment, or in recovery.

The healing energies of Reiki are pure in nature and form. When combined with a sincere desire to be healed, by both practitioner and client, a deep cleansing of their physical, emotional, mental and spiritual selves is achieved. While it is ultimately the free will of each client to desire this healing to occur, one should keep in mind that this energy awaits the positive, productive empowerment of the client before their intentions will be met. It's for this reason that I would recommend to all my clients that they be attuned and learn Reiki themselves. Additionally, the harmony and balance of the Reiki practitioner plays an instrumental role in allowing the Reiki energy to flow freely into the client. If a Reiki practitioner has physical, mental, emotional or spiritual energy blockages, these can inhibit the natural flow of Reiki from practitioner to client. By working on improving yourself, your capabilities for helping others are improved. As your awareness and ability increase, so too does your awareness of why you are here and what your purpose is.

Usui's system of healing offers far more than simply the ability to heal yourself and others. It is a *part science part spiritual art*' practice that allows you to reach complete self-awareness and spiritual understanding. When you practise Usui's techniques daily, you will strengthen and deepen your understanding of what Reiki is and the nature of existence itself.

The first step in transforming back into your real self involves self-healing first and foremost. When you have healed yourself on a physical level, you are prepared to work on healing your mental and emotional layers. Once you have achieved this level of physical, mental and emotional balance and have activated your core being, you will be prepared for discovering the spiritual and mystical nature of the Universe and yourself.

Committing yourself to Usui Reiki does not mean committing yourself to Reiki. It means committing yourself to yourself and striving to follow and understand your own unique path in life. And as we transform ourselves from the inside out, Reiki transforms with us, because Reiki *is* us.

CHAPTER 3
THE ORIGINS OF REIKI

66 *A jug fills drop by drop.* 99 - **Buddha**

There are different versions regarding the history of Reiki that have been told, some more fanciful than others. The following history of Reiki is based upon known facts relating to its origins.

Reiki was thought to have originated from Japan roughly one hundred years ago however, the symbols used in Usui Reiki are far older and date back several thousand years to ancient Tibet and Buddhism. Mrs. Hawayo Takata brought Reiki from Japan to the West in 1937, where she continued to teach a number of people to Reiki Master-Teacher level. These 22 Reiki Masters then proceeded to spread Reiki further. If it was not for the efforts of Takata and her 22 Master students, Reiki would not have spread throughout the world and would still be practiced in secret by a small number of practitioners to this day.

Mrs. Takatas' story was spread by these 22 Reiki Masters and her version of its origins were printed and shared in many early books on Reiki. However Takatas interpretation of the history of Reiki was not wholly accurate. Takata also related Reiki to Jesus Christ rather than Buddha to make Reiki more appealing to a Western audience. Because of these changes the original myths surrounding Reiki spread with the practice and are still taught by many Reiki Masters to this day. Truth is we do not have a great deal of information about Dr. Usui or the true Divine origins of Reiki. What we can say is that this version of Reiki was re-discovered by Master Usui during deep meditation. Mikao Usui created his own organisation for Reiki, called the Usui Reiki Ryoho Gakkai, and in order to practise the healing techniques of Reiki without government interference and licensing, the organisation decided to become a secret society to preserve the Reiki teachings. Due to this, it was very difficult for anyone to learn Reiki at this time and many Japanese people had to travel to America to learn Reiki techniques and practices. Because of this, the Reiki practiced throughout the Western world and Japan has evolved into what we practice today.

Mikao Usui worked hard throughout his life and had a deep interest in expanding his science and spiritual based knowledge. His studies included medicine, psychology, religion and the art of divination among many others. His interest in science and spirituality led him to become a member of the *'Rei Jyutu Ka'*, a group who strived to understand and develop human psychic abilities, as he attempted to use his broad based knowledge and experience to discover the true capabilities of the human mind and the real purpose of life.

Usui learned multiple languages so he could study ancient religious and spiritual texts and eventually discovered a process by which one could achieve a higher state of consciousness which would provide one with an understanding of their true life purpose. This altered state of being was known as *'An-Shin Ritus-Mei'*, pronounced *'On Sheen Dit Sue May'*. When one achieves this level of consciousness, they develop a state of perpetual inner peace, no matter what may be happening around them. This state automatically maintains itself in a cycle without any effort or input from the individual.

From this state of being one begins a journey of self-discovery and realization which helps one understand their true purpose and unique destiny in life in an on-going quest towards achieving full spiritual enlightenment. Mikao Usui dedicated his life to achieving this state of mind and being and through the practice of Zazen Meditation, he continued his journey towards enlightenment. After a few years of practise, Usui had not been successful in his quest and upon further guidance from his spiritual teacher, Usui began a dangerous practice that brought him very close to death.

Dr. Usui went to Kutama Yama Mountain to fast and meditate, a process that lasted 21 days and saw him become weaker and weaker as time passed. Upon the 21st day, physically and mentally weak and on the verge of death, a powerful energy suddenly struck Usui's head, which caused him to instantly fall to the ground unconscious. Upon his awakening, Usui realized that he now felt revitalized and was now filled with a powerful energy that he had never before experienced. Usui became aware of a frequency of energy that had opened his dormant mind to a new level of consciousness which had improved his awareness.

Overjoyed by the awakening he was experiencing, Usui ran down the mountain with excitement and stubbed his toe on a rock on the way down. Naturally, he held his painful toe in his hand and it was at this point that Usui realized he had also been gifted with the ability to heal. Usui felt the healing spiritual energy of Reiki emanating from his hand and flowing into his painful toe automatically, which subsequently removed all sensation of pain from his body. At this moment, Usui realized he had been awakened to the ability to heal. After years of research, hard work and searching, Usui had achieved a spiritual awakening.

Usui had an extensive knowledge in many medical, philosophical, religious and spiritual disciplines and after further experimentation on his family members, Usui established his new system of healing. Known in English as *'The Usui Reiki Treatment Method for Improvement of Body and Mind'*. There were other Reiki healing methods already being practised in Japan during Usui's time, however this method of healing is unique to Master Usui, as he discovered how to tap into this specific frequency of Divine healing energy through his own knowledge, efforts and determinations.

In April 1922, Usui moved to Tokyo and started the healing society known in English as the, *'Usui Reiki Healing Method Society'*, and he also opened a Reiki clinic in Harajuku, Aoyama, Tokyo, where he taught classes and gave treatments to the general public. From this point, knowledge of Usui's abilities began to slowly spread throughout Japan.

The first and lowest degree of his training was called *'Shoden'* which was separated into four levels. Loku-Tou, Go-Tou, Yon-Tou, and San-Tou. When Mrs. Takata taught this first level, which in the West we refer to as Reiki Level I, she combined all four levels into one. The next degree was called *'Okuden'* (Inner Teaching) which we refer to as Reiki Level II today. The next degree was called *'Shinpiden'* (Mystery Teaching), which is what we call master level in the Western world. However Master Usui did not originally have a Master Symbol as part of his healing system. Usui had only three symbols, with the Reiki Master Symbol being added into the practice some time later. Usui's original symbols are the same three symbols currently used in the West in Reiki Level II, the power symbol, the emotional and mental symbol and the distance healing symbol.

In 1923, a great earthquake devastated Tokyo and killed more than 140,000 people. Earthquake Kanto caused over half of the houses and buildings to crumble to the ground. Many people were left homeless, injured, sick and in mourning, so Usui took it upon himself to treat as many of these victims with Reiki as he could and began teaching others how to give Reiki at this time to help him heal the sick and injured. At times, Usui would give Reiki to four people at a time, lying on the ground and channelling through his two feet and hands simultaneously.

After this, demand for Reiki became so great that Usui outgrew the clinic he opened, resulting in a bigger clinic being built in Nakano, Tokyo, in 1925. Usui's reputation as a gifted healer spread throughout Japan and to the attention of the Emperor. Usui began to travel so he could teach and treat more people and in his time spread Reiki to more than 2,000 students. Usui also initiated twenty Reiki Master Teachers who were given the same understanding and ability to channel Reiki as he had learned to use it.

For his work helping others, Dr. Usui was awarded a high merit award, the *'Kun San',* by the Japanese Government and continued to practise and teach Reiki until his death on March 9th, 1926, when he suffered from a fatal stroke. After Dr. Usui died, his students erected a memorial stone next to his gravestone. Mr. J. Ushida, a Reiki Master Teacher trained by Dr. Usui, took over as president of the Usui Reiki Ryoho Gakkai and was responsible for creating and erecting the Usui Memorial stone that can still be visited in Japan to this day.

CHAPTER 4
USUI MEMORIAL INSCRIPTION

The following translation is reproduced here with the permission of Richard Rivard and is available at www.threshold.ca/Reiki/usui_memorial_translation.html

Translation of the Usui Memorial at Saihoji Temple, Tokyo

© Copyright 1998-2011 Emiko Arai and Richard Rivard -- Please feel free to share this document with others – as is, with no changes --

Since a friend in Japan sent us pictures of the Usui memorial in the spring of 1996, we had wanted to put this web page up. Many other projects got in the way and we didn't get a good close-up of the monument until our friend Shiya Fleming brought back some good photos in July 1997. Emiko and I spent several days going through the old dictionaries she had and I was very happy at the end to compensate her with Reiki Master training for her part in the process. Finally, I felt we had completed enough to present this to others.

This is a fairly literal translation of the Usui memorial, as we wanted you, the reader, to get as close a rendition to plain English as possible, without any paraphrasing. This allows you to decide how you would rephrase sentences and paragraphs.

All comments in *(brackets)* are either our translations of previous kanji *(in quotations),* or our explanation of previous words. Please note: there are no periods or paragraphs on the original, so we have added these in to make it easier to read. Also, as in all translations, we had several choices of words for each kanji and tried to pick what we felt best depending on the content. Our thanks to Melissa Riggall and Miyuki Arasawa for their corrections offered and to later translations shared with me.

Although this location does contain the remains of Usui Sensei's wife – Sadako; son – Fuji; and daughter – Toshiko, it only has a part of Sensei's remains. The Saihoji site is not the original resting place of the Usui family. The original grave site was set up a year after Sensei's death in a Tendai Buddhist graveyard near what is now Nakano station. Then in 1960 the entire graveyard was moved to the Saihoji Temple site in order to make way for an extension to the main subway line. This was confirmed by Saihoji Temple workers in 2009. Sensei's living students *(there were several at the time of this writing in 1998)* said he was a Tendai Buddhist all his life *(the Saihoji temple is a Jodo Shyu (Pure Land) Buddhist temple)*. There is also a small private shrine elsewhere in Tokyo - donated by an Usui doka *(student)* - that holds some of the original remains of Usui, as well as the original Usui Concepts *(Precepts)* wall hanging, and the original large photo portrait of Sensei taken by Dr. Hayashi *(who was an amateur photographer)*. This was set up shortly after his death in 1926.

Please share this information with all, but we ask you to leave this introduction portion and copyright with it. For pictures and location of the memorial, please visit my Saihoji Temple pages.

I would like to express my gratitude to all those who have offered changes and corrections to the translation.

===== translation begins =====

"Reihou Chouso Usui Sensei Kudoko No Hi"
Memorial of Reiki Founder Usui Sensei's Benevolence

(The kanji at the top of the memorial reads, from right to left: "Reihou" - spiritual method, Reiki method; "Chouso" - founder; "Usui"; "Sensei" - teacher; "Kudoku" - benevolence, a various (pious) deed; "no Hi" - of memorial, a tombstone, a monument - this is also what the first line in the main text says)

It is called 'toku' that people experience by culture and training and 'koh' that people practice teaching and the way to save people. *('koh' + 'toku'= 'kudoku; Kou = distinguished service, honor, credit, achievement; Toku = a virtue, morality)*

Only the person who has high virtue and does good deeds can be called a great founder and leader. From ancient times, among wise men, philosophers, geniuses and ? *(a phrase that means - very straight and having the right kind of integrity)*, the founders of a new teaching or new religion are like that. We could say that Usui Sensei was one of them.

Usui "Sensei" *(literally "he who comes before", thus teacher, or respected person)* newly started the method that would change mind and body for better by using universal power. People hearing of his reputation and wanting to learn the method, or who wanted to have the therapy, gathered around from all over. It was truly prosperous. *(by "therapy" is meant the Usui Reiki Ryoho - Usui ancestral remedy - of his Usui-Do teachings, including the 5 principles).*

Sensei's common name is Mikao and other name was Gyoho *(perhaps his spiritual name)*. He was born in the Taniai-mura *(village)* in the Yamagata district of Gifu prefecture *(Taniai is now part of Miyama Village)*. His ancestor's name is Tsunetane Chiba *(a very famous Samurai who had played an active part as a military commander between the end of Heian Period and the beginning of Kamakura Period (1180-1230). However Hirsohi Doi revealed at URRI 2000 that Tsunetane was a son of Tsuneshige, who was 1st son of Tsunekane, and that Usui Sensei is descended from Tsuneyasu, the 3rd son of Tsunekane)*. His father's name was Uzaemon *(this was his popular name; his given name was Taneuji)*. His mother's maiden name was Kawai.

Sensei was born in the first year of the Keio period, called Keio Gunnen *(1865)*, on August 15th. From what is known, he was a talented and hardworking student. His ability was far superior. After he grew up, he visited the western world and China to study *(yes, it actually says that, NOT America and Europe!)*. He wanted to be a success in life, but couldn't achieve it; often he was unlucky and in need. But he didn't give up and he disciplined himself to study more and more.

One day he went to Kuramayama to start an asceticism *(it says "shyu gyo" - a very strict process of spiritual training using meditation and fasting.)* On the beginning of the 21st day, suddenly he felt one large Reiki over his head and he comprehended the truth. At that moment he got Reiki "Ryoho" *(This term originally meant ancestral remedy or therapy)*.

When he first tried this on himself, then tried this on his family, good results manifested instantly. Sensei said that it is much better to share this pleasure with the public at large than to keep this knowledge to our family *(it was customary to keep such knowledge in the family to increase their power)*. In April of the 11th year of the Taisho period *(1922)* he moved his residence to Harajuku, Aoyama, Tokyo. *(this is next to the Meiji Outer Gardens and the huge Aoyama Cemetery)*. There he founded "Gakkai." *(a learning society)* He taught Reiki Ryoho. *(According to his student Tenon-in, who in 2003 is 106, Sensei was teaching his spiritual method simply called "his method," referred to by his students as "Usui-Do." It was based upon the concepts he wrote called Usui Reiki Ryoho)*. People came from far and near and asked for the guidance and therapy and many shoes lined up outside of the building. *(In Japan you take your shoes off at the door)*.

In September of the twelfth year of the Taisho period *(1923)*, there were many injured and sick people all over Tokyo because of the destruction brought with the Kanto earthquake and fire. Sensei felt deep anxiety. Every day he went around in the city to treat them. We could not count how many people were treated, helped and saved by the efforts of

18

Usui. During this emergency situation, his relief activity was that of reaching out his hands of love to suffering people. His relief activity was generally like that. *(Mr. Hiroshi Doi was told that Sensei would actually lay on the ground and give Reiki from his hands and feet to at least 4 people at a time).*

After that, his learning place became too small. In February of the 14th year of the Taisho period *(1925)*, he built and moved to a new one *(a dojo or training hall)* outside Tokyo in Nakano. *(Nakano is now part of Tokyo)*. Because his fame had risen still more, he was invited to many places in Japan, often. In answering those requests, he went to Kure, then to Hiroshima, to Saga and reached Fukuyama. *(Fukuyama was also the location of Sensei's creditors - his final trip was mainly to meet with them)*. It was during his stay in Fukuyama that he unexpectedly got sick and died. He was 62 years old. *(In Western terms, Sensei was 60 - born August 15, 1865; died March 9, 1926 as per his grave marker; however, in old Japan, you are "1" when born and turn another year older at the start of the new year)*.

His wife was from Suzuki family; her name was Sadako. They had a son and a daughter. The son's name was Fuji who carried on the Usui family *(meaning the property, business, family name, etc. Born in 1908 or 1909, at the time of his father's death Fuji was 19 in Japanese years. We learned that Fuji may have taught Reiki in Taniai village. According to the Usui family grave stone, the daughter's name was Toshiko, and she died in September 23, 1935 at the age of 22 in Japanese years. Sensei also taught his wife's niece who was a Tendai Buddhist Nun. As of this writing (2003) she is still alive - approximately 108).*

Sensei was very mild, gentle and humble by nature. He was physically big and strong yet he kept smiling all the time. However, when something happened, he prepared towards a solution with firmness and patience. He had many talents. He liked to read and his knowledge was very deep of history, biographies, medicine, theological books like Buddhism Kyoten *(Buddhist bible)* and bibles *(scriptures)*, psychology, jinsen no

19

jitsu *(god hermit technique)*, the science of direction, ju jitsu *(he also learned Judo from Jigoro Kano, according to Tenon-in)*, incantations *(the "spiritual way of removing sickness and evil from the body")*, the science of divination, physiognomy *(face reading)* and the I Ching. I think that Sensei's training in these, and the culture which was based on this knowledge and experience, led to the key to perceiving Reiho *(short for "Reiki Ryoho")*. Everybody would agree with me. *(The origins of the Usui-Do system are now known to be from Taoism and Shinto brought to Japan from China, probably around the 5th century.)*
Looking back, the main purpose of Reiho was not only to heal diseases, but also to have right mind and healthy body so that people would enjoy and experience happiness in life. Therefore when it comes to teaching, first let the student understand well the Meiji Emperor's admonitory, then in the morning and in the evening let them chant and have in mind the five precepts which are:

First we say, today don't get angry.
Secondly we say, don't worry.
Third we say, be thankful.
Fourth we say, endeavour your work.
Fifth we say, be kind to people.
(My friend Emiko Arai was very firm about the above wording.)

This is truly a very important admonitory. This is the same way wise men and saints disciplined themselves since ancient times. Sensei named these the *"secret methods of inviting happiness"*, *"the spiritual medicine of many diseases"* to clarify his purpose to teach. Moreover, his intention was that a teaching method should be as simple as possible and not difficult to understand. Every morning and every evening, sit still in silence with your hands in prayer *(gassho)* and chant the affirmations, then a pure and healthy mind would be nurtured. It was the true meaning of this to practice this in daily life, using it, *(i.e. put it into practical use).* This is the reason why Reiho became so popular. *(see my document on the Usui Precepts for more on this.)*

Recently the world condition has been in transition. There is not little change in people's thought. *(i.e. it's changing a lot)* Fortunately, if Reiho can be spread throughout the world, it must not be a little help *(i.e. it's a big help)* for people who have a confused mind or who do not have morality. Surely Reiho is not only for healing chronic diseases and bad habits.

The number of the students of Sensei's teaching reaches over 2,000 people already *(This number may also include the students' students).* Among them senior students who remained in Tokyo are carrying on Sensei's learning place and the others in different provinces also are trying to spread Reiki as much as possible. *(Dr. Hayashi took title to the dojo in November, 1926 and together with Admiral Taketomi and Admiral Ushida, re-located it to his clinic in Shinano Machi in 1926, and ran it as a hospice.)* Although Sensei died, Reiho has to be spread and to be known by many people in the long future. Aha! What a great thing that Sensei has done to have shared this Reiho, which he perceived himself, to the people unsparingly.

Now many students converged at this time and decided to build this memorial at his family temple in the Toyotama district *(this was originally in a Tendai graveyard near what is now Nakano station. The grave sites were all moved to the Saihoji Temple in 1960 in order to make way for an extension of the main subway line)* to make clear his benevolence and to spread Reiho to the people in the future.

I was asked to write these words. Because I deeply appreciate Mikao Usui's work and also felt moved by those people who felt honored to be a student of Sensei Usui, I accepted this work instead of refusing to do so. I would sincerely hope that people would not forget looking up to Usui Sensei with respect.

(The location of the burial plot and memorial may have been the work of the Admirals and the URR Gakkai. Usui Sensei was confimed by his living students Tenon-in and Suzuki-sensei to have been a devout Tendai until his death. Yet the Saihoi temple is a Pure Land sect or Jodo Shu Buddhist temple.)

Edited by "ju-san-i" *("subordinate third rank, the Junior Third Court (Rank) - an honorary title),* Doctor of Literature, Masayuki Okada.

Written *(brush strokes)* by Navy Rear Admiral, "ju-san-i kun-san-tou ko-yon-kyu" *("subordinate third rank, the Junior Third Court (Rank), 3rd order of merit, 4th class of service" -- again, an honorary title)Juzaburo Ushida (also pronounced Gyuda).*

Second Year of Showa *(1927),* February

CHAPTER 5
THE DEVELOPMENT OF REIKI

❝ *Each morning we are born again. What we do today is what matters most.* ❞ - **Buddha**

Our knowledge of Reiki has further developed since Mikao Usui discovered the healing art. Before Dr. Usui passed to the other side, Chujiro Hayashi, who was a close friend and student of Dr. Usui, was requested to open his own Reiki clinic and to expand and develop Reiki based upon his experience as a medical doctor in the Navy. Chujiro Hayashi opened a school and clinic called *'Hayashi Reiki Kenkyukai'*, the *'Hayashi Reiki Institute'*, and proceeded to develop the Reiki hand positions we know today. This helped to ensure each individual patient received a balanced treatment by focusing Reiki upon each of the seven main Chakras. Patients could also opt to lie down on a therapy bed, rather than be seated on a chair as was originally the case. This allowed each patient to experience a much deeper level of relaxation and a more effective treatment.

After the Japanese attack on Pearl Harbour and because of his knowledge of Hawaii, Chujiro Hayashi was asked by the Japanese military to provide information relating to the location of enemy targets in Honolulu. Hayashi refused to share any information with the Japanese Government because he could not bring himself to be part of such slaughter. As a result, Hayashi was declared a traitor by the Japanese Government. This caused Chujiro to lose respect within the community and he and his family were ostracized from Japanese society. As a result of his loving heart, Hayashi felt his only solution was ritual suicide, which Hayashi willfully carried out. In honorable tradition, Chujiro Hayashi passed away on May 11th, 1940 and should be remembered for his loving contribution to humanity and his sacrifice. Including Usui and Hayashi, Hawayo Takata too played an important role in the development and spread of Reiki.

HAWAYO TAKATA

Hawayo Takata, who was instrumental in spreading Reiki to the Western world, shared her story of the years leading up to her experience with Reiki and what alterations she made to Usui's system of healing after becoming a Reiki Master herself.

Hawayo Takata was born on December 24th, 1900, on the small island of Kauai, Hawaii, and was the daughter of Japanese immigrants. Her father worked within a sugar cane plantation and Takata soon married the plantations bookkeeper, where she was also employed. After her husbands' death in October 1930, Hawayo Takata was left to raise their two children on her own. The hard work and stress of having to raise her children while also working soon took its toll on Takata.

After five years of hard work, Takata developed severe abdominal pains, a lung condition and suffered from a nervous breakdown. Shortly after this, one of her sisters died, leaving Takata with the responsibility of travelling back to Japan to deliver the sad news to her parents. After breaking the news to her parents, Takata's poor health diminished further and she had developed gallstones, asthma, appendicitis and a cancerous tumour. Rather than endure a surgical operation, Takata instead made the decision to visit the Hayashi Reiki Institute in search of an alternative solution.

While Hawayo Takata was unfamiliar with the practice of Reiki, she was nevertheless surprised by the diagnosis she received from Hayashi's Reiki clinic. Her diagnosis closely matched that of the physicians at the hospital where she initially attended. As part of her treatment for her illnesses, Takata received a daily session from two Reiki practitioners for a number of months. During this time, Takata had the opportunity to experience the healing energy of Reiki as a client. Amazed by the heat and sensations she experienced, Takata questioned what was happening and how the healers were able to perform such seemingly magical acts and showed a keen desire to learn.

This was the beginning of Takatas' journey into Reiki and the catalyst that would eventually spread Reiki throughout the world.

After four months of regular daily treatments, Mrs. Takata had become progressively better until she was eventually healed. Hawayo Takata stated that she was healed of all her illnesses at the Hayasho Reiki Institute, including her cancerous growth. Amazed by this, Takata asked if she could learn the Reiki healing techniques herself and had received her First Degree attunement from Dr. Hayashi in 1936. After working in the Hayashi Reiki Institute for a period of one year, Mrs. Takata received her Second Degree attunement, after which she returned back to Hawaii in 1937. Shortly after this, Chujiro Hayashi and his daughter followed Takata to Hawaii in 1937 and helped to establish the first Reiki clinic in the country.

In February of 1938, Chujiro Hayashi attuned Hawayo Takata as a Reiki Master. After this, Hawayo Takata continued to practice Reiki in Hawaii and opened several more Reiki clinics there where she gave treatments and attuned students up to Second Degree level. Takata became a well-known and respected healer through her clinic and travelled to the Americas and various other parts of the world where she gave treatments and taught others how to channel Reiki for themselves.

It wasn't until thirty two years later in 1970 that Takata started attuning people to the level of Reiki Master. Takata also proceeded to change some of the original aspects to how Chujiro Hayashi taught her, simplifying and standardising her treatments so that each one would be the same. Takata also removed the traditional Japanese Reiki Techniques which were passed from Dr. Usui to Hayashi and then to herself. It is believed that Hawayo Takata was the one who added the Reiki Master Symbol to this Reiki healing method and who changed the attunement process by creating a different attunement for each level. This effectively combined the multiple attunements for each level into one single attunement which saved time and simplified the entire process.

Mrs. Takata passed away in December of 1980 and had successfully attuned twenty-two Reiki Master Teachers who proceeded to teach others and spread Reiki around the world. Today, it is estimated that there are over 1,500,000 Reiki Masters around the world and well over 4,500,000 practitioners. Thanks to the Reiki Masters of days gone by for spreading this gift throughout the world, these numbers continue to grow! Thanks to Takata, and all those respected Masters before her, Reiki is slowly but surely changing the world for the better, one small spiritual step at a time.

REIKI IN THE PRESENT

Reiki is practised in many different countries all over the world and this gift is now passed on from Master to student for a far more reasonable fee. Reiki is a spiritual energy and while our experience and understanding of ourselves evolves, so does the art and science of Reiki. Today, there are many different types of Reiki which are available to learn. Many of which however, do not have any direct lineage to the traditional form practised and taught by the original masters.

One of the newer forms of Reiki include Karuna Reiki, which is a powerful addition to traditional Reiki that integrates and complements the original teachings of Dr. Usui. A lesser known practice in the world is Reiki Tummo, which completely opens the central energy channel running up the spine and activates the Kundalini. Reiki Tummo provides the first steps towards becoming an enlightened Yogi and is one form of Reiki every serious spiritualist would be advised to learn.

Reiki Tummo involves tapping into the energies of the earth, our root Chakra and our heart and will significantly increase any and all other forms of energy channelling. There are currently somewhere over 100 different types of Reiki being practised in the world today, many being offshoots of the original Usui Reiki. These include Tibetan Reiki, Angelic Reiki, Rainbow

Reiki, Atlantean Reiki, Kundalini Reiki, Fire Reiki, Tummo Reiki, Sun Li Chung Reiki, Eastern Reiki, Golden Age Reiki, Ascension Reiki, and many others.

Those knowledgeable in these various forms report that each version of Reiki does work in its own way, however each strain of energy feels different from the traditional healing practice, as taught by Dr. Usui and his descendant masters. These other versions are available to you if you wish to explore them and while it may be difficult to know which way to turn and which path to walk, using your intuition to help guide you would be the advice I would give.

I would also personally recommend that every serious Reiki practitioner learns one of the forms of Reiki that focus on your Kundalini and give serious thought to becoming attuned to Tummo Reiki. Once you read the hidden meaning behind the Kanji for the word Reiki, which is included later in this book, you will have a deeper understanding as to why learning a form of Kundalini Reiki is very important if you wish to reach your full spiritual potential. When we awaken and activate our bodies Kundalini energy, we greatly increase our connection to the Divine Source.

There will no doubt be additional strains of Reiki being developed as time advances and extra add-ons to the traditional system of Reiki, as taught by Dr. Usui. Personally, I feel that the Traditional form of Usui Reiki, the added use, flexibility and power of Karuna Reiki and the additional empowerment given through fully activating our Kundalini with Reiki Tummo, is all that is necessary to help one discover their own path in life and fulfill ones spiritual purpose.

Experience is the real teacher of all things, and whichever form of Reiki you do choose to discover, the better placed you will be to understand the many mysteries of both the outside world and your true inner self. Just remember that intellectual experience is very different from spiritual experience.

THE BENEFITS OF REIKI

Unlike modern day medicine and pharmaceuticals, Reiki works on restoring balance and harmony on all levels, mind, body and spirit, rather than simply relieving symptoms or masking the cause of those symptoms. Some of the benefits are as follows:

- Alleviates pain
- Accelerates the body's natural rate of healing
- Improves the immune system
- Increases energy levels
- Balances emotions
- Dissolves energy blockages and promotes natural balance between the mind, body and spirit
- Creates deep relaxation and helps remove stress and tension from the body
- Helps with insomnia and aids better sleep
- Reduces blood pressure
- Clears the mind and helps improve concentration and focus
- Removes toxins and free radicals from the body
- Assists ones spiritual growth and psychic development
- Compliments all other forms of healthcare
- Alleviates the side affects that may be experienced from drugs and medical treatments

You don't have to be ill to receive a Reiki treatment as there are always areas of ones overall health that can be improved. At the most basic level, Reiki helps our mind, body and spirit come into harmony and unison. As one advances through the higher levels of Reiki, it becomes apparent that this energy can be used for far greater purposes than healing alone.

OTHER THINGS REIKI CAN TREAT

Reiki can be used for any issue you can think of, whether physical, emotional, mental or spiritual in nature. It can effectively treat migraines, asthma, skin conditions, flu and colds, ulcers, arthritis, anxiety, back problems, depression, low self-esteem, poor self-confidence, shyness, memory loss and forgetfulness and literally any other condition. You can be treated when receiving chemotherapy to help alleviate the side effects of that treatment, you can use it in hospitals, when you are pregnant, when on medication, when using any other form of therapy and when pregnant.

Remember that Reiki can also be given to all animals, insects, plants, flowers, crystals and stones, your drinking water or bath water, broken electrical items, or anything else you can think of. The only limit when using Reiki is the limit you place upon your own imagination.

WHEN NOT TO GIVE REIKI TO SOMEONE

Reiki is always safe and there are only a couple limited situations when it would be advised not to treat someone with Reiki. If someone has a finger accidentally cut off, or has broken a bone, then these are two occasions when it would not be a good idea to give that person Reiki. The reason for this is because Reiki will drastically accelerate that persons natural healing rate. And in the case of lost fingers or broken bones, this could cause them to heal prematurely before there's time to have the finger surgically re-attached, or their bone realigned in a cast or plaster.

HOW REIKI WORKS

While spiritual healing traditions have been practised for thousands of years, to this date science has been unable to explain how it works. Some things are beyond the understanding of our limited human brain. Therefore we must use our non-physical senses, or those that exist above our every day five physical senses, to experience and understand Reiki fully. We know how to tap in and use Reiki and we know what Reiki can do and while there are theories for how it works, truth is we do not know exactly how it does what it does. In the manual Mikao Usui gave his students, he states the following:

66 *...I've never been given this method by anybody nor studied to get psychic power to heal. I accidentally realized that I have received healing power when I felt the air in mysterious ways during fasting. So I have a hard time explaining exactly what it is, even though I am the founder. Scholars and men of intelligence have been studying this phenomena but modern science can not solve it. But I believe that day will come.* **99**

Sometimes imagination is more powerful than knowledge and whatever our mind can conceive, we can achieve. What can be said about Reiki is that it activates, balances and harmonizes our Chakras and personal energy field. This is the same energy field that has been photographed using Kirlian Photography. Illnesses and diseases of the physical body are often rooted within our energy system and when we allow our energy field to become too low, physical consequences manifest in the form of dis-ease.

There are some things in life that are beyond the understanding of our primitive human brain and intellect. As time progresses, we will learn to develop a deeper understanding of ourselves, the cosmos and how we can interact with its many energies through feeling them. Or otherwise being intuitively aware of them. True knowledge comes from experience and the further we develop our connection to the Reiki energies, the deeper our knowing will become.

In time, one comes to realize that some things can not be understood on an intellectual level. They have to be experienced and felt through the Heart Chakra. It's experiencing Reiki and feeling its power that leads us towards this deep knowing within our hearts and it's from the Heart Chakra that we can connect to the Divine Source of Reiki and creation itself.

THE ETHICS OF REIKI

One of the most important of all Reiki ethics is to ask if someone wishes to receive a treatment or attunement, as free will is one of the most important attributes for personal growth and spiritual development. There will be those who do not wish to be healed for personal reasons and others whose current spiritual path may not be in resonance with Reiki. Regardless of your own thoughts, opinions and beliefs that Reiki can only be a good thing for someone, it is nevertheless not your right to force your opinions or beliefs on anyone else. Respect the wishes of others and remember the following ethics of Reiki:

- Always ask your clients permission to channel Reiki to them
- Never take advantage of a client or abuse your position of trust
- Never offer diagnosis for a client's illness unless you are a qualified doctor
- Never offer Reiki as a cure to disease
- Never use energy channeling for negative purposes

The quality and strength of the Reiki you are able to channel is limited by the human constraints you place upon it. Those who become the best healers are those who strive to become the best channel for Reiki and this is done by removing ones ego from their healing treatments and creating balance and harmony within themselves. When you fully open and surrender yourself to the Divine Source you enter your most resourceful state of being.

By allowing the Divine Source to work through us without interfering with its flow of energy, we ensure the energy of Reiki always goes to where it's needed most and does so in full flow. As human beings, we do not have the knowledge or authority to be aware of why people may be suffering with an illness or disease. In spiritual terms, there is a reason and blessing for even the worst of circumstances. Our task is to become aware of what that blessing is. Being able to channel Reiki should be seen as the first step before learning to surrender ourselves completely to the Divine Source and in doing so, we open ourselves to becoming the most efficient channel. When we surrender our complete being to the Divine Source of Reiki we become one with it and it's here our true power lies.

MONEY AND EXCHANGE FOR GIVING REIKI

The concept of receiving an exchange for giving Reiki treatments is an important one, not only for the person giving a Reiki treatment, but for the individual client receiving it. Balance is an important aspect of everything in life and Reiki treatments are no different. While a practitioner may place little value on money, or not feel comfortable receiving money from their clients in exchange for giving them Reiki, it is important to view this from the perspective of an *'exchange of energy'*. The practitioner gives energy, in the form of Reiki, and the client balances the equation by returning energy in some form.

There will be clients that would feel uncomfortable not exchanging money for Reiki services and if you refuse to accept this *'exchange of energy'*, you can leave clients with negative energy because they may feel indebted to you for providing a free service. It can also stop clients from returning to you for future treatments for fear of being a burden to you.

There are other ways of exchanging energy that do not need to include an exchange of money. If you don't accept money for giving a Reiki treatment, appreciate the importance of allowing your clients to give, as well as receive, as this helps to create an energetic balance within that client. To balance the equation, be happy to receive a token gesture from a client who wishes to give something back. This token gesture could be in the form of a donation, a card, a crystal, a plant, a stone from their garden, or anything else. The item itself is not important. It is the gesture that is appreciated and making sure your client does not harbor feelings of guilt for taking and not giving. If a client is adamant that they must give you something and they only have money to give, it would be advised to kindly accept this *'exchange of energy'* for your clients own piece of mind. You can always donate the money to a local charity if this makes you feel better which makes everyone a winner.

Charging money for Reiki is completely acceptable and there is absolutely nothing wrong with it. It is simply a personal decision whether to do so or not. You have to successfully complete Second Degree Reiki before you qualify for Public Indemnity Insurance and are able to safely offer your services to the public. If you plan on completing your Second Degree Reiki and offering your services to the public, as a general rule of thumb, charge roughly the same as others in your area are charging for reiki treatments or a professional massage.

Expect your Reiki sessions to last anywhere between 45-minutes to an hour-and-a-half, or longer should you wish. It is quite common for professional Reiki Practitioners to start their fees off low and to gradually increase the amount they charge per-session as their confidence, experience and reputation grows.

CHAPTER 6
THE REIKI PRINCIPLES

66 *Your life is a blank screen. What you see on it is merely a projection of your inner self. Being aware of your projections is the first step towards self-understanding.* 99 **- Ricky Mathieson**

Reiki provides each practitioner with a key. This key aids ones understanding of the spiritual path they are currently following in their life. Do not think of any of the Reiki techniques as rules. They are not rules. They simply provide guidelines to the practitioner and offer a tried and tested framework for how one can connect to the Divine energies. Reiki acts only as a tool to help you on your journey of self-discovery and it places no demands or expectations upon you. You are wholly responsibility for your own thoughts, actions and beliefs and Reiki is not here to tell you how to think or act or what to believe. Its purpose is only to help *"guide"* you towards where you should be for your highest and greatest good.

An important part of that guidance has been given to us in the Principles of Reiki. The Reiki Principles are not laws or rules on how to be kind and civilized. They are fundamental keys that all students of life would be advised to adopt. When we understand the deeper purpose behind the Reiki Principles and integrate them into our daily way of thinking and behaving, we automatically prepare our bodies and minds to be the purest channel possible for the energy of Reiki.

The Reiki Principles written upon Usui's memorial stone offer us guidance for our journey ahead and Usui advised his students to practice them twice daily. Once in the morning and once at night. Usui emphasized a great degree of importance on incorporating the principles into our daily lives and for good reason. The Reiki Principles are not rules of behaviour. They are virtues that show one how to live a peaceful and harmonious life.

<u>The Reiki Principles</u>
First we say, today don't get angry.
Secondly we say, don't worry.
Third we say, be thankful.
Fourth we say, endeavour your work.
Fifth we say, be kind to people.

An alternative and wider known version of the Reiki principles are as follows:

The secret art of inviting happiness.
The miraculous medicine off all diseases.
Just for today, do not anger.
Do not worry and be filled with gratitude.
Devote yourself to your work. Be kind to people.
Every morning and every evening, join your hands in prayer.
Pray these words to your heart and chant these words with your mouth.
Usui treatment for the improvement of body and mind.

Another commonly written description of the Reiki Principles, that are quite different from the message behind the original Principles, are as follows:

Just for today, do not anger,
Just for today, do not worry,
Honour your parents, teachers and elders,
Earn your living honestly,
Show gratitude to every living being.

Dr. Usui asked his students to live by these Principles daily and their relevance are just as important today as they were during his time. Incorporating The Reiki Principles into your daily life can be a valuable part of your practice. Not only will it help to balance and improve your life, it will contribute towards improving your Reiki channelling abilities. As we become more consciously aware of their importance and make the effort to integrate them into our daily lives, they become part of us, helping us understand their deeper relevance to the practice of Reiki and how they can improve our lives and treatments.

A deeper explanation of each of the 5 Reiki Principles are as follows:

Just for today, do not anger...

Suppressing and ignoring anger is unhealthy, however venting it is no better. Anger is not something you have to *"let out"* in an aggressive way in order to avoid erupting from the inside. Outbursts of anger only fuel the fire and contribute towards making your anger problem worse. As quoted from Buddha, *"Holding on to anger is like grasping a hot coal with the intent of throwing it at someone else. You are the one who gets burned."*

True power doesn't come from venting anger and directing this towards others. This is bullying. The truth is, venting anger is an indication one lacks control over their emotions and feelings. Anger is often directed towards others so one may feel in control of the situation in front of them because they are not in control of themselves. However, if you can't control yourself or handle opposing viewpoints, you will lose a valuable opportunity for self-growth and realization, as your anger will be greatly inhibiting your ability to understand yourself, other people and events from an objective viewpoint. Others will be more willing to listen to you and accommodate your needs if you communicate in a respectful way and by doing so, you will be better able to understand the root cause of your anger through healthy communication. Within every situation that makes you angry lies an opportunity for self-discovery.

Like all your other emotions, anger is a message from yourself. Your emotions are simply a tool for helping you understand what goes on around you and within you. If you can learn not to react to your anger and think about what is causing that anger when it arises, then this can be the first step towards understanding and finding a solution. We should be grateful for being shown the opportunity to transform our weakness and understanding how to grow from them. All feelings of anger can be transformed by dealing with them constructively.

Energy attracts the same energy and the people and situations that are drawn into your life are done so by yourself. We all attract the experiences we need for personal growth into our lives and if we do not learn the deeper meaning and lesson behind that experience, we will continue to attract similar experiences into our lives until we become self-aware. Everything in your life is simply a mirror of yourself. This gives you the opportunity to take a look at yourself and come to a deeper understanding of what is hiding inside. It is often an unwillingness to see what we don't like within ourselves that makes us feel and express our anger as a way of not having to deal with the feelings brought with it.

Of course, we are all human and anger is a natural impulse. We may not always be able to control the situations we find ourselves in, or how they make us feel. However we *can* always choose how we express our anger and we *can* express our anger without being verbally or physically abusive. Even if someone is pushing all our buttons, we always have a choice for how to respond to that input.

It is important to remember that anger hurts *you* more than it hurts the person you are venting it at. Your relationships, your judgement, your career, your emotions, your health, and your state of mind, are all negatively affected when you do not control your response to anger. Never suppress any of your emotions. This is not healthy and your emotions are there for good reason. Rather than trying to suppress your anger, make it your goal to express it in constructive ways. If you do not and don't understand what your anger is trying to show you about yourself, then you will continue to attract similar people and events into your life that cause you to feel more and more anger until you understand the lesson behind that anger. Don't allow your emotions to define you as the person you are. Use them as a tool to define yourself.

❝ When you think everything is someone else's fault, you will suffer a lot. When you realize that everything springs only from yourself, you will learn both peace and joy. ❞ **– His Holiness the 14th Dalai Lama**

Just for today, do not worry…

In the same way as our response to anger, we can *choose* not to worry. Worry is linked to fear and is another highly toxic state of being, for our mind, body and our spiritual selves. Worrying about something does not empty today of its sorrow. It empties tomorrow of its strength. One guarantee in everyone's life is change. We change from the moment we are born right up until the moment of our physical death. And there are only two ways to confront change. We can fear it and worry about it. Or we can embrace it. Every situation we experience in life offers us a new opportunity for self-growth and if we can learn to see every situation as an opportunity to grow, we can learn to let go of worry and embrace change and the uncertainty that is often brought with it.

Every emotion and feeling has an energy attached to it which holds either positive or negative energy and like attracts like in the unseen world. Our minds create our reality, as our reality is simply a projection of our own mind. It is quite often the case that we come to realize that there was no need to worry about a future situation once we are in that situation. So worrying about it serves to only direct negative energies towards that point in time. Again, much like anger, worry can affect your relationships, your judgement, your career, your emotions, your health, and your state of mind. Don't play the *'what if'* game and try to guess the future. Be content and focused upon the here and now. This helps us prevent worrying about either the past or the future.

If you receive something that you consider to be a negative experience, remember that it is only a lesson and there is something to be learned about yourself in that lesson. There is no such thing as a positive or negative experience. An experience is simply an experience. It is only our own minds that perceive something to be either positive or negative. And that is the reality we create for ourselves through our own choice. Never regret anything and never worry about anything. If what happens to us is perceived as good, it's wonderful. If what happen to us is perceived as bad, then it's an experience to take value from.

❝ *If you can solve your problem, then what is the need of worrying? If you can not solve it, then what is the use of worrying?* **❞ – Shantidiva, 8ᵗʰ Century Buddhist Monk**

Take into consideration the following ancient Zen Buddhism and Taoist story and contemplate its meaning:

❝ There is a Taoist story of an old farmer who had worked his crops for many years. One day his horse ran away. Upon hearing the news, his neighbours came to visit. *"Such bad luck"*, they said sympathetically.

"Maybe", the farmer replied. The next morning the horse returned, bringing with it three other wild horses. *"How wonderful, such good luck"*, the neighbours exclaimed.

"Maybe", replied the old man. The following day, his son tried to ride one of the untamed wild horses and was thrown to the ground and broke his leg. The neighbours again came to offer their sympathy on his sons poor misfortune. *"Maybe"*, answered the farmer.

The day after, military officials came to the village to draft young men into the army. Upon seeing that the farmers son's leg was broken, they passed him by. The neighbours congratulated the farmer on his sons good fortune and how well things had turned out. *"Maybe"*, said the farmer. **❞**

The meaning of this ancient story has already been mentioned. There is no such thing as a positive or negative experience. An experience is simply an experience. It is only our own minds that perceive something to be either positive or negative. The truth is, the Divine order and path of our lives is there to show us truths and learn lessons. And whether we may *think* a certain situation is either good or bad, we really don't know what that situation is going to bring us in the future. Sometimes bad things have to happen in order to create something better for us further down the line. However if we do not see this, then similar scenarios will continue to repeat themselves in the future until we see and understand the lessons to be learned behind them. By keeping your thoughts, mind and energy focused upon the positive, or the potential positive, you ensure that every experience in your life can only have a positive outcome.

Be filled with gratitude...

It is important to be filled with gratitude and to appreciate the many things we already have in life and to realize that there lies a blessing and opportunity for further personal growth in every situation. Focusing on only the positive, or potential positive, in life, helps us raise our energetic vibration and attract only peace and abundance.

Rather than worrying, taking what you have for granted and constantly wanting what you do not have, learn to appreciate what you already have. Simply being given the opportunity to be alive is the rarest and most precious of all gifts because with that, we are given the opportunity to direct our own lives and to influence the world around us. If we can trust that everything that happens in our life is there to give us an opportunity to further develop ourselves, we will automatically magnetically attract what we truly need the most into our lives.

When we realize that we already have enough, we will be truly rich in all aspects of our life. If we work on the Universal Law of Attraction constructively, we can achieve any and all of our goals more easily, receiving an abundance of all good things into our lives and being in gratitude for these blessings. Remember, our minds create our reality, and whatever our thoughts conceive, we will receive. So be careful what you think/wish for. You will likely receive it.

❝ *Be thankful for what you have and you'll end up having more. If you concentrate on what you don't have, you will never, ever have enough.* ❞ **– Oprah Winfrey**

There are those of us who have had a far more difficult life than others and no matter what is said or done, I can sympathize why some people may find it very difficult to be grateful for what they have received. If you can't be content with what you have received, be thankful for what you have escaped.

Devote yourself to your work…

Another of Dr. Usui's original Reiki Principles is to *"Devote yourself to your work"*. However this should not be confused with necessarily devoting yourself to your job or career. This is devoting yourself to the *great work*, or in other words, your Divine purpose in this life. We all have one and it is your responsibility to discover what that purpose is and Reiki will help guide you in that direction. For the purposes of self-discovery and realization of truth, I would recommend everyone continue their journey up through the levels to Reiki Master Teacher. Even if you teach nobody else, the most important person you can ever teach is yourself.

Devoting yourself to improving the self, through meditation and connection to your spirit and beyond, is the devoting Dr. Usui speaks of. We can not devote ourselves to our true purpose in life if we are unable or unwilling to first be honest with ourselves. The fact you are reading this Reiki Guidebook now is evidence of your desire and quest towards that honesty. Only when we are willing to pull back the illusionary curtain that exists between our eyes and the spiritual world, can we then begin to understand the true nature of the world, ourselves and our purpose in it. It is then our chosen path in this physical life becomes clear to us, helping us see the lessons that must be learned from the experiences we are given. Inviting this honesty into your life will improve your relationship with those around you and ultimately improve your relationship with your spiritual self and the Divine consciousness that interconnects us all. Through devoted action, we learn how to balance our lives and create harmony between our inner and outer world.

When we are in balance and harmony with ourselves, we are then in a position to achieve our maximum potential for helping to create balance and harmony in the lives of all those around us. When we relinquish the need to always be in control, we allow our physical bodies and mind the opportunity to connect to the deepest aspect of our self. Our spirit. It is once we achieve this level of connection and live a life of truth and not illusion, that we align ourselves with our higher purpose in life. The main message behind this principle is to *devote yourself to discovering that truth of purpose.*

66 *A teacher is never a giver of truth. He is a guide, a pointer to the truth that each student must find for themselves.* 99 – **Bruce Lee**

Be kind to people…

Dr. Usui's system of Reiki was primarily intended to help one upon their personal journey of self-discovery by helping to improve their life, growth and spiritual development. The Reiki principles are intended to help one achieve that inner peace and happiness.

The Reiki Principle of *"Be kind to people",* offers deeper benefits to every individual who incorporates this practice into their daily lives until it becomes an integrated part of their existence. People deserve to be treated with kindness. However these principles offer us a deeper awareness and understanding as to why it's important to be kind towards other people for our own sake. We will all come across people who are on opposing paths to our own and there will be individuals that think, speak and act in ways that we would consider to be inappropriate. Rather than be quick to label and stereotype someone, keep in mind that everyone you meet is fighting their own personal battle in life. And when kindness is shown, kindness is returned to you.

Understanding that everyone is on their own personal path of self-discovery is important and just because one may have awakened and elevated themselves to a higher level of existence, does not mean they are better or more evolved than the next person. Remember that every person who comes into our lives, whether for a reason, a season or a lifetime, does so in order to provide us with a deeper insight into ourselves. This gives us the opportunity to share, learn and grow.

Without having those individuals enter our lives, even for a moment, we would lose that priceless opportunity for growth. Take what is currently happening on a planetary scale, with the wars, suffering, death and destruction that inflicts our planet. While we may not like such a thing, it serves the purpose of helping us understand what is important to us as individuals and what needs to be changed.

Any person that directs anger, jealousy, hatred, unkindness, or any other negative emotions, towards us, is doing so because they are experiencing their own personal troubles. It is easy to be nice to people who treat you well. The real test is to be nice to people who treat you badly. By responding to such negative influences in a negative way, not only do we negatively contribute to that persons troubles, we also create negative energy within ourselves as a result.

Take the following story about the *"The Buddhist and the Villager"* and contemplate its meaning:

❝ Buddha was speaking in a village square one day when one of the villagers started to verbally abuse him.

Buddha paused and said to the man, *"If you offer me a piece of paper and I refuse to accept it, what happens to that piece of paper?"*

After some thought the villager replied, *"Why, it stay with me, of course."*

Buddha smiled gently. *"And that is exactly what I am doing with your abuse,"* he said. *"I am not accepting it. Therefore it stays with you".* 99

No matter what sort of verbal abuse is directed towards you from another, it can not hurt you unless you allow it to. And by reacting to negativity with more negativity, not only do you not help the person venting that abuse, you also suffer the negative personal emotional, mental, physical and spiritual consequences of allowing that abuse to incite a negative response within your own mind and body. As Martin Luther King, Jr. was quoted saying, *"Darkness can not drive out darkness. Only light can do that. Hate can not drive out hate. Only love can do that."*

Only with love can one help others see the errors of their ways. Retaliating with more anger or hatred only lowers yourself to the same level of consciousness as those who would direct it towards you. This contributes towards the endless cycle of anger, hatred and separatism amongst humanity.

Remember that every situation you find yourself in presents an opportunity to achieve greater understanding and personal growth. And if everybody reacted to negativity with love, the world would be a far more peaceful place. Keep in mind the *Universal Law of Karma*. Whether you believe this or not, it still applies to you. Karma is a little like a restaurant without menu's. You will always get served exactly what you deserve.

Whatever energy you project into the world is the exact same energy you will get back, whether you are conscious of this or not. If you direct anger, worry and disbelief into the web, it's vibration travels back through you in time. By projecting positive energies into the ether, such as love, peace and belief in ourselves and the Divine higher power that guides us, we are able to connect our inner heart deeper to the source of creation. That starts and ends in your Heart Chakra. Your emotional connection to love in its free form.

Honour your parents, teachers and elders. (*A modern addition to the Reiki Principles*)

This part of the Reiki Principles were not part of Dr. Usui's original Principles for daily living. They were created and added at a later date, however they are an important point to address. Having honour for your parents, your teachers and your elders means having respect for these individuals, what they give you and offer you and what can be learned from such people. What having honour for your parents, teachers and elders should not mean however, is fulfilling an obligation or keeping an agreement between them and yourself if this does not resonate with your own intellectual thoughts, feelings and beliefs.

Believe nothing, no matter where you read it, or who said it, unless it agrees with your own reason and your own common sense. The mother of all teachers is direct experience and whatever you are taught or told is simply a relative truth based upon your parents, teachers and elders own personal life experiences. While there can be much wisdom to be had from such people, you should **ALWAYS** keep an open mind and **QUESTION EVERYTHING**. Including what is laid out within the pages of this manual.

Do not believe in anything simply because you have heard it. Do not believe in anything simply because it's believed by the majority. Do not believe in anything simply because it has been written. Do not believe in traditions that *tell* you what to believe and control your behaviour. And do not believe in anything merely on the authority of your parents, teachers and elders. But only after observation and analysis, when you find that anything agrees with reason and common sense and is conducive to the good and benefit of one and all, then accept it and live up to it.

Reiki is about taking control and responsibility for yourself, your own unique purpose and your own unique path in life. See it and use it as a tool to be your own shepherd and do not blindly follow the path others would have you walk down. Every human being is the shepherd of their own existence. No one else. The only truth you can rely upon in life is an absolute truth. And that comes from direct first-hand experience.

66 *The best teachers show you where to look, but don't manipulate what you see.* 99 - **Ricky Mathieson**

Reiki is as much about preparing your own state of mind and being than it is about learning and practising Reiki. By working on your own self-control and developing your own awareness, understanding and perceptions about yourself, others and life in general, you are laying the necessary foundation upon which to build Reiki into your life further. Not only will this aid your personal development, it will drastically improve your abilities to channel an increasing flow of Reiki as you allow yourself to *become* Reiki. Or to become one with the creative source that exists everywhere and in everything.

CHAPTER 7
CHANGING THE REIKI PRINCIPLES

❝ The mind is the source of happiness and unhappiness. ❞
- Buddha

One persons rule is another persons guideline and Reiki demands that you follow no strict rules. Reiki is a tool and a guide to help you discover yourself and uncover absolute truth. If something doesn't resonate with you or doesn't work for you, change it to work for you better. It's important to remember that the Reiki Principles are not laws or rules, neither are they moral obligations. They are guidelines for leading a spiritually balanced and harmonious life with oneself and ones surroundings.

Reiki is a spiritual pursuit and a personal path of growth and development, with every practitioner and Master having a different point of view, varying life experiences and a unique way of relating to the universe and everything in it. What seems appropriate and logical to one Reiki practitioner will not be a view that is necessarily shared by another, as our spiritual path in this life is unique and personal to each of us. Likewise, with regards to The Reiki Principles, they may be changed slightly, or completely, to a daily affirmation that you feel more respondent to.

The important thing is that your Reiki Principles are positive, that you are in a receptive state of mind when focused upon them and that they come from a pure and loving heart.

While I can appreciate the deeper meanings and purpose behind the original Reiki Principles, they do not resonate with me on a personal level. Therefore I have changed the Reiki Principles to a version I feel more comfortable with, while keeping them as close to the original meaning and purpose as possible.

❝ Just for today... (*helps one focus on the present and not the past or future*)

I am at peace,
I believe in myself,
I am appreciative and grateful,
I work hard on myself,
I am kind towards other people,
I feel love and compassion for myself and all living things. ❞

As well as this version feeling right for me, I feel it's important to change the first two principles to something more positive, as the original version is focused on a negative, rather than a positive. The Science of Neuro Linguistic Programming teaches us that the language we use influences how we think and feel. Therefore we behave in accordance with our language.

Our minds are programed by the language we use, or the words we think and speak. NLP teaches us that our minds are not able to differentiate between *"Today i will be angry"* and *"Today I will NOT be angry"*, as you are programming the mind with a negative word...*'angry'*. Therefore changing the words 'anger' and 'worry', in the original Reiki Principles into their positive replacements, *'peace'* and *'believe'*, we are programming the mind with positive rather than negative language. And of course, *'Love and Compassion'* are one of the *'three fundamental keys'* to helping you reach your full Reiki channelling potential.

Have you ever noticed that your words closely match your actions? Your words help create those actions. Change the words you use and you can change how you think, feel and behave. You are your brains own programmer. You choose how to think and subsequently feel. So many people are looking for happiness and love and the irony is, this is not something one truly finds in the outside world. This is something one must focus on becoming on the inside. It's been hiding inside you all along. And by projecting the energies of happiness and love inwards, towards your whole heart, or intending to create happiness and love in your life while chanelling Reiki towards this intention, you can literally programme yourself to achieve this state of being. Humans are pretty unique that way. We are the one species that have the ability to change ourselves into someone completely different in an instant. Your thoughts are directly responsible for not only the energy you create, but the energy you attract into the cycle of your life. So choose your words wisely and be mindful of your thoughts. They become your life.

WHY THE REIKI PRINCIPLES ARE IMPORTANT

The Reiki Principles were very important to Dr. Usui and remained a daily part of his practice and teachings. Dr. Usui realized that good health was so much more than being physically free of illness, disease and disorder. Having good health was also a point of view and an attitude, two things which can be changed through habitual programming of the mind.

It's important that each of us are healthy mentally, emotionally and spiritually as well as physically. By focusing the mind on only positives and repeating your Reiki Principles on a daily basis, you are habitually programming yourself to be psychologically healthy. A fact the Science of NLP and The Law of Attraction confirms for us. And a healthy mind is necessary if we are to achieve physical, emotional, mental, and spiritual balance and harmony in our lives.

Everything in the Universe is energy at the atomic level, each thing consisting of a different frequency or vibration. The energy we project into the Universe returns to us. This is not a spiritual theory, this is an established law of physics.

66 *Your thoughts are the architect and your emotions the builder. Karma dictates that the energy of the thoughts and emotions you choose to express will be returned to you.* 99 - **Ricky Mathieson**

When we come to realize that everything in our outer world is a direct reflection of what goes on in our inner world, we take that first step towards discovering how to create and shape our reality as we see fit. Keep this in mind and choose your thoughts and affirmations wisely. You will likely become them.

CHAPTER 8
THE HUMAN CHAKRAS

❝ *Health shows in your physical body while well-being shows in your energy body. Therefore being well involves more than being physically healthy. Wellness is a state of body, mind, energy and spirit. Wellness therefore, is a state of being. Are you well?* ❞
- **Ricky Mathieson**

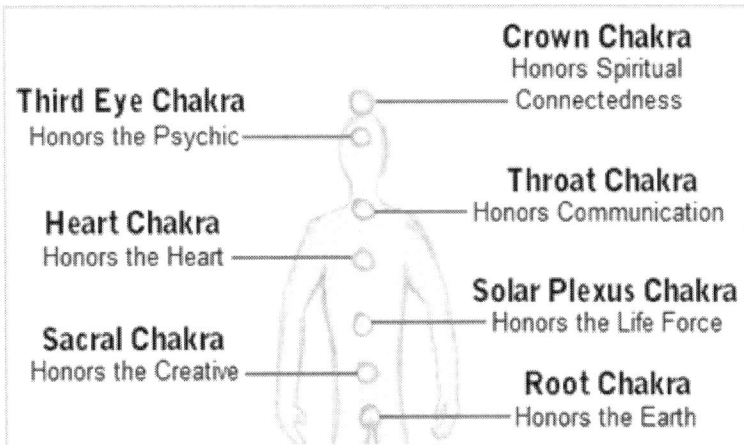

Crown Chakra
Honors Spiritual
Connectedness

Third Eye Chakra
Honors the Psychic

Throat Chakra
Honors Communication

Heart Chakra
Honors the Heart

Solar Plexus Chakra
Honors the Life Force

Sacral Chakra
Honors the Creative

Root Chakra
Honors the Earth

Science has shown us that all living life forms have an energy field around their bodies and when the body is healthy, this energy field can be observed at its fullest. The energy flowing into our bodies is the life-force energy that keeps us alive and healthy and when we further open our connection to it and use it for healing, our energy bodies become balanced and healthy.

This energy field is also commonly referred to as the aura and consists of seven different layers of energy that surrounds the human body. Each layer of our energy field is connected to one of our seven main Chakras that run down the middle of our body. 'Chakra' is the Sanskrit word meaning wheel and while the original system of Reiki is not traditionally associated with the Chakras, as the Chakra system was traditionally an Indian concept that was not used in Japan, it has been incorporated into the practice of Reiki. Mikao Usui had a wide knowledge in many different energy disciplines and knew that focusing Reiki on the Chakra system would help to balance and expand the energies of each one. While chanelling Reiki to our Chakras can help to balance them and promote well-being, it can also help us to open our psychic abilities and improve our spiritual development.

Each Chakra is a non-physical center of energy that constantly absorbs and expels energy from inside and around you. In total, there are around 365 of these energy centers throughout the human body. Here we focus upon the seven main Chakras which run down the center of your body.

  7. Crown Chakra – Violet – Top of the Head
  6. Third Eye Chakra – Indigo – Between the eyebrows
  5. Throat Chakra – Blue – At the throat
  4. Heart Chakra – Pink – At the center of the chest
  3. Solar Plexus – Yellow – At the naval
  2. Sacral Chakra – Orange – at pelvic bone above genitals
  1. Root Chakra – Red – at the end of the tailbone

Each of the seven main Chakras running down the middle of our body relates to a different layer of our energy field and our Chakras are the emotional centers of those outer energy layers. By regularly cleansing and healing our bodies Chakras, we also cleanse and heal our outer energy layers. It's these energy layers that influence our physical, emotional and mental health, so ensuring each energy layer is balanced and healthy is of prime importance if we are to be balanced and healthy in body, mind and spirit.

If you are not aware and in control of your bodies energy field, you are leaving a large part of your health to chance. This is the basis of how Reiki is able to heal us, by topping up our bodies with an increased flow of healthy life-force energy.

THE 7 LEVELS OF THE HUMAN ENERGY FIELD

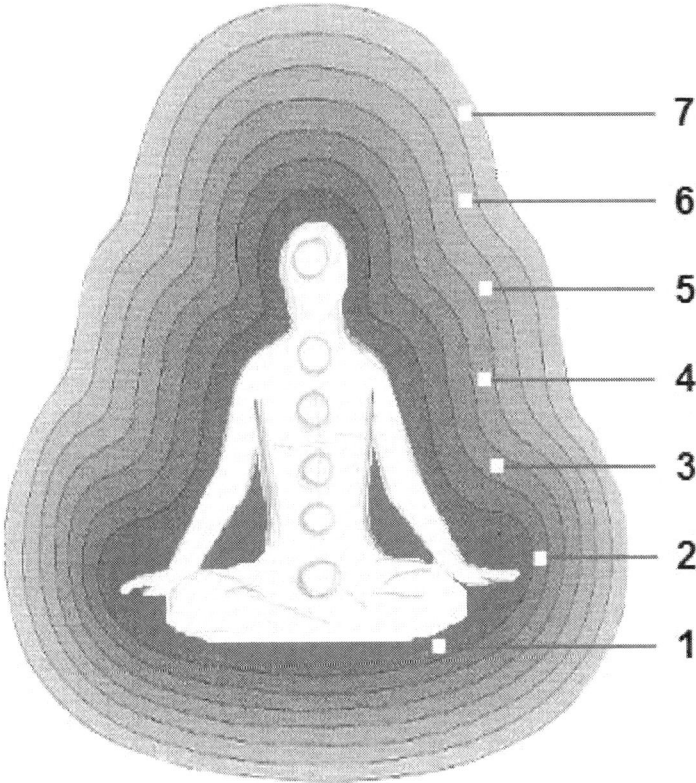

Each of our seven main Chakras corresponds to a different layer of our energy field. When the Chakras of our body are balanced and healthy, the energy field that surrounds us is healthy too. Each layer of the human energy field relates to the following:

1. **Etheric** – Field upon which the body tissue is formed. Your physical health is attached to this layer.
2. **Emotional** – Feelings about ourselves. Developing unconditional Love for the self will heal this energy layer.
3. **Mental** – Logical mind. Using positive words and creating positive thoughts helps heal this energy layer.
4. **Astral** – Record of all past experiences, including relationships, childhood and past lives. Developing unconditional Love for others will heal this energy layer.

5. **Template** – Divine Will and structure. Gaining a sense of Truth and Purpose will heal this energy layer.
6. **Celestial** – Divine Love. Developing unconditional Love for all of creation will help to heal this energy layer.
7. **Causal** – Divine Wisdom. Remembering the perfection in all of life will heal this energy layer.

Being aware of our body's' different fields of energy and what each relates to is an interesting aspect of energy healing that one should be aware of. While Byosen scanning *(explained later)* and your own intuition will help lead you to where your hands need to go, you should keep in mind that the best place to position your healing hands will not always be directly touching the physical body. It could be several feet above the body, relating to which aspect of the self is most in need of healing.

The densest part of this energy field is location number one, which is closest to the physical body and each additional layer is a higher vibration of energy. Layer seven is the highest vibration of energy that surrounds the physical body. The size of the energy field around each person is different and depends upon the health and balance of their seven main chakras.

Our surrounding energy field reacts to how we think and feel and our physical, mental and emotional health are all impacted by this energy field. This puts a lot of importance on balancing our mind and controlling our thought processes, as we can literally think ourselves into positive or negative health. Our seven energy layers are closely integrated and influenced by one another and this energy field ripples down to our physical body, causing it to be either healthy or unhealthy. Because of this, being of good health involves far more than simply being physically healthy. It involves a healthy and balanced state of mind and a positive attitude and outlook on life.

Once you become sensitive enough to feel this field of energy, you can use your hands and the Byosen Scanning Technique to feel where to place your hands during a Reiki treatment. Using the hands to feel this energy will help give a better understanding of the life-force energy that gives us life. One of the easiest and most effective ways of sensing this field of energy is by using one palm to sense the energy emanating from the other. Once your hands increase in sensitivity, you will be able to sense the auras of the people around you, as well as your own. Peoples energy fields can be anywhere from a couple meters to over 25 meters in size. So when you are mingling with friends, family and the general public, you are also mingling your energy field with their energy field. This makes cleansing your own energy field especially important, as negative energies from those around you can influence every aspect of your health and well-being.

While these are the seven main chakras focused upon when channelling Reiki, there are actually hundreds of chakras located throughout the human body. Each one connected through energy pathways known as Meridians, which allow the flow of energy around and through our bodies. As well as each acupuncture point being one of the smaller chakras found in the body, there are also several hundred spiritual chakras that exist above the head. Achieving balance and harmony in all of these spiritual Chakras is the goal of spiritual enlightenment.

The Reiki hand positions, detailed in the following chapter, have been designed to ensure each of the bodies seven main Chakras receive a balanced energy treatment. This is especially useful for Reiki beginners who may not be able to intuitively sense the energy fields of others. However keep in mind that Mikao Usui encouraged all of his students to work on developing their intuitive skills when channelling Reiki.

CHAPTER 9
WESTERN REIKI HAND POSITIONS

❝ *You don't have a soul. You are a soul. You have a body.* ❞ -
C.S. Lewis

HAND POSITIONS WHEN GIVING SELF-TREATMENTS
The Front – Head Positions

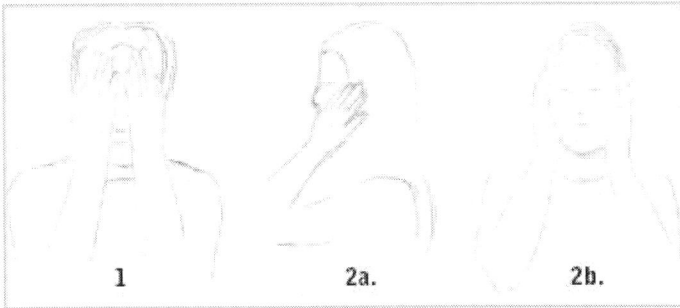

1. Over the eyes.
2a. Over the cheeks, thumbs just under each ear.
2b. Alternate 2nd position, with fingers over temples.

The Back – Head Positions

3. Back of the head, over the occipital ridge.
3a. Alternate 3rd position, for back of the head.

Neck, Chest, Torso – Body Positions

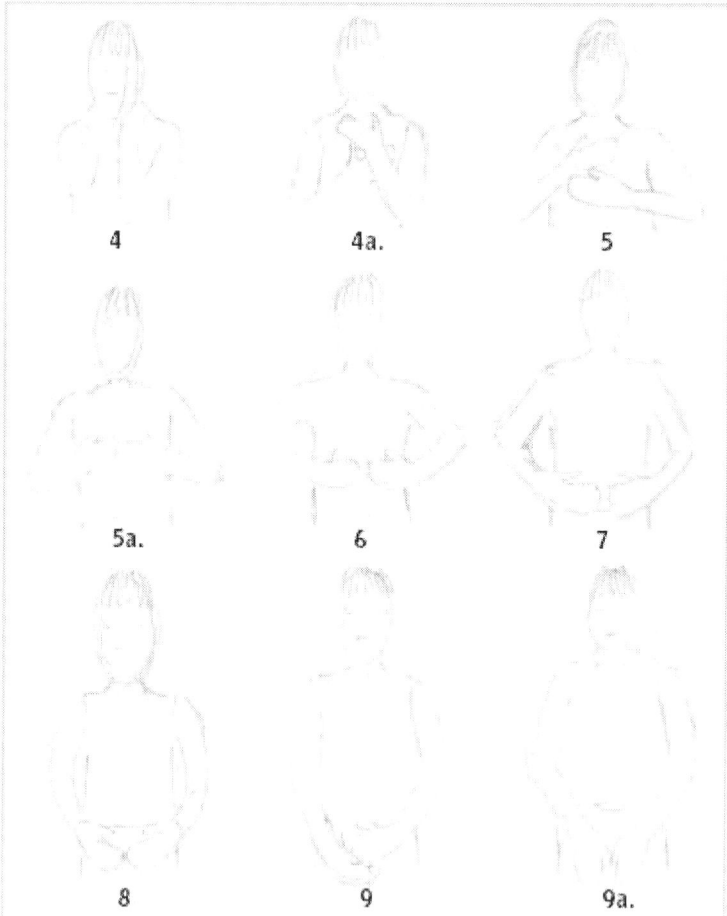

4. Over the throat.
4a. Alternate throat position.
5. Over the heart and Breastbone. *(self-treatments only)*
5a. Alternate 5th position. *(self-treatments only)*
6. Over lower ribs below the breast.
7. Over the middle of the abdomen.
8. Over the pelvic bones on the lower abdomen.
9. Hands in the center above the pubic bone. *(not touching the genital area)*
9a. Alternate 9th position over pubic area. *(self-treatments only)*

Knees, Ankles, Feet – Positions

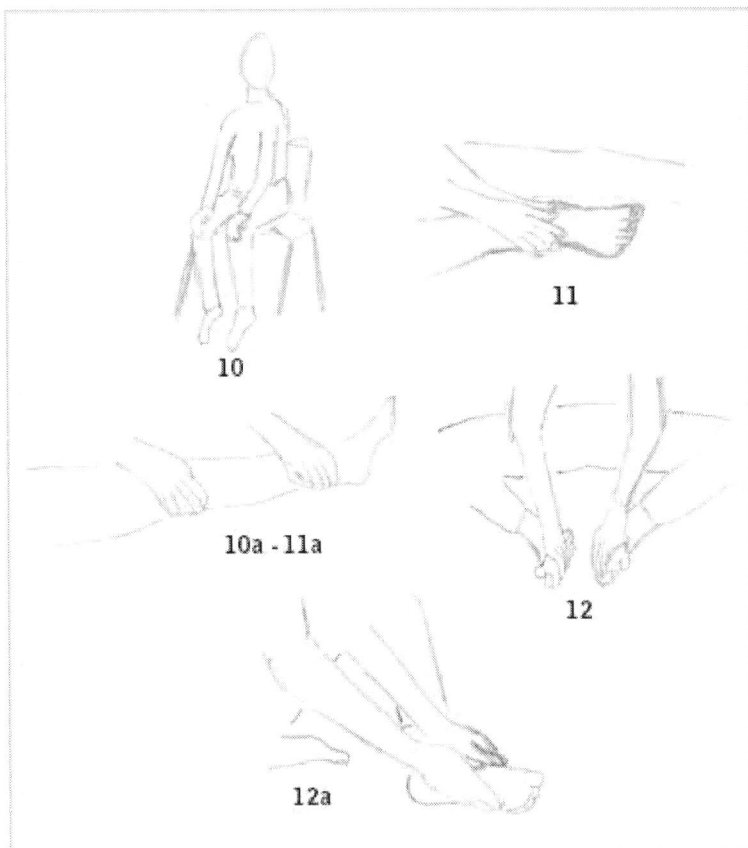

10. Front of both knees
11. Front of both ankles
10a – 11a. Knee and ankle done together, one leg at a time.
12. Bottom of both feet.
12a. Bottom of one foot then the other.

These are the hand positions used in Usui Reiki for giving yourself a self-treatment. Keep in mind that appropriate hand positions must be used when treating others to avoid touching inappropriate areas of the body. Using hands, however, is not a *necessity*. You need only your heart and your mind.

POSITIONS WHEN GIVING OTHERS TREATMENTS

Front Of Body Hand Positions

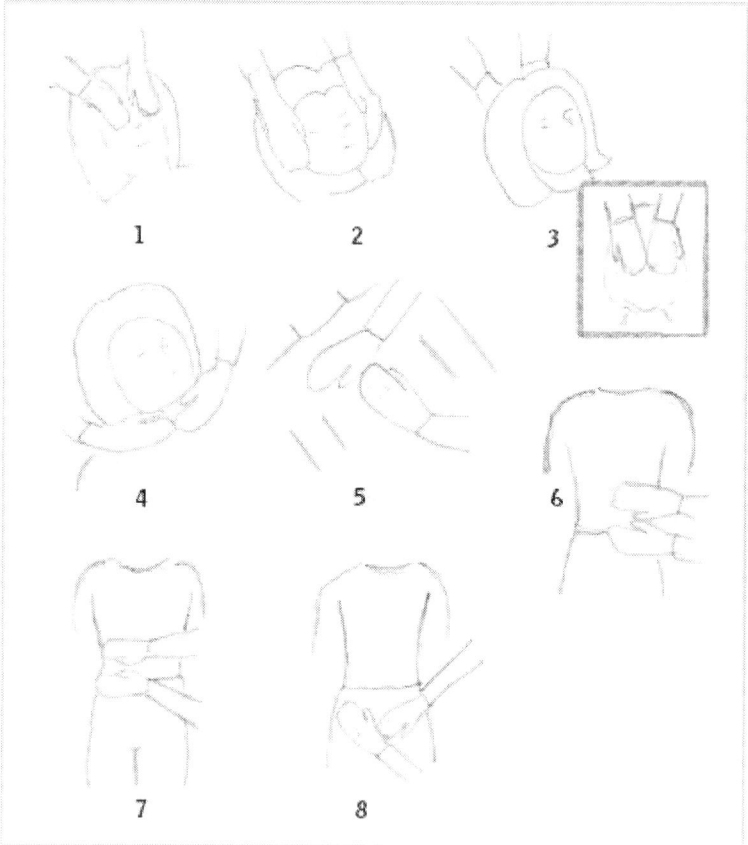

1. **Third Eye Chakra**, with your hands over the eyes.
2. Side of the head, each palm on each temple area.
3. **Crown Chakra**, under the head, gently tilt your head to one side & slide one hand under first.
4. **Throat Chakra**, keep your hand a couple inches away and apply no touch or pressure.
5. **Heart Chakra**, place one hand on top of the other to avoid touching the breast area if necessary.
6. **Solar Plexus Chakra**.
7. **Sacral Chakra**

8. **Root Chakra**, keep your hands on the thighs and either away from the genitals, or hovering above them.

Back Of Body Hand Positions

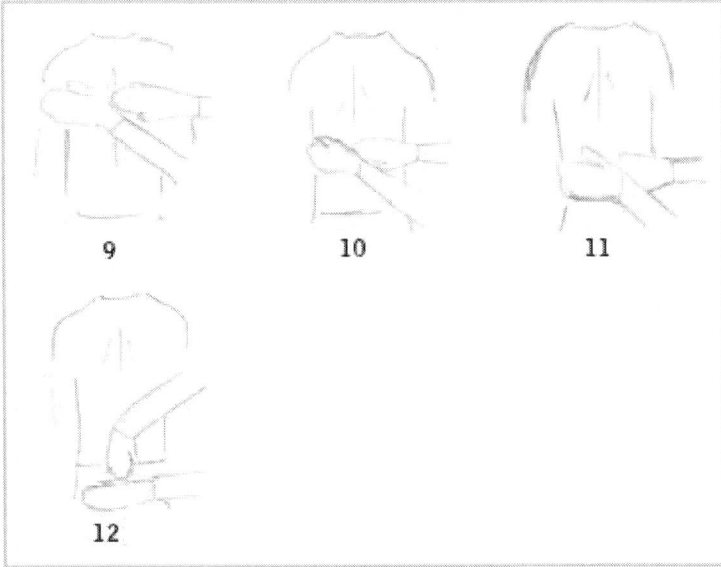

9
10
11

12

9. Shoulders.
10. Middle Back.
11. Lower Back.
12. Coccyx, also referred to as the tailbone, the final point of the vertebral column.

These are the 12 hand positions that were later added to Reiki and taught by Chujiro Hayashi. You will notice however, that the first 8 hand positions on the front of the clients body cover all 7 of the main Chakras. Therefore it is not necessary to turn your client over mid-way through a Reiki treatment to place your hands upon their back. Not only is it not necessary, but it will also interfere with your clients level of relaxation and state of mind. Reiki is intelligent in nature and it can be sent over long distances using only the mind and without any hands at all, as is taught during the Second Degree Reiki Attunement. You will discover with practise that the Reiki energy flows to exactly where it's needed, regardless of where you place your hands. How you conduct your treatments however, is up to you.

Once you have finished with the hand positions, remember to place your hands on your clients knees and then feet, if they are comfortable with this, and ground them.

HAND POSITIONS FOR SPECIFIC BLOCKAGES

When giving yourself a self-treatment, or treating anyone else, there are different ways this can be done. You can either use your own intuition, the Byosen Scanning method as encouraged by Dr. Usui, or if you have not yet built up sensitivity in your palms and can not feel where Reiki energy is needed, you can use Chujiro Hayashi's method and treat each part of the body using the various self-treatment hand positions. If using the hand positions, each hand position on the body relates to the following areas:

1. **Third Eye Chakra,** Cup eyes and face – Heals the Lower Brain, Eyes, Sinuses, Nose, Mouth, Face Muscles, Frontal Lobes of Brain, Spine, Pituitary Gland.
2. Ears – Heals the Ears, Upper Neck, Blood Flow To Brain and Upper Spinal Vertebrae.
3. **Crown Chakra,** Crown of Head – Heals the Upper Brain, Pineal Gland, Scalp, Cerebral Cortex, Skull.
4. Back of Head – Heals the Cranial Bones, Cerebral Spinal Fluid, Upper Spinal Column.
5. Shoulders – Heals the Lower Neck, Shoulders, Mid Cervical Vertebrae.
6. **Throat Chakra,** Throat – Heals the Lower Jaw and Mouth, Thyroid, Para Thyroid, Oesophagus, throat, Upper Lungs, Upper Arms, Digestive Tract.
7. **Heart Chakra**, Heart – Heals the Thymus, Heart, Lungs, Upper Thoracic Vertebrae, Circulation.

8. **Solar Plexus Chakra**, Solar Plexus – Heals the Stomach, Liver, Gallbladder, Spleen, Adrenal Glands, Pancreas, Mid Thoracic Vertebrae, Upper Abdominal Area, Solar Plexus, Ribs.
9. **Sacral Chakra** – Heals the Reproductive Organs, the Urogenital System, Testicles, Legs, Transverse Colon, Mid Abdominal Area, Kidneys, Small Intestines.
10. **Root Chakra** – Heals the Ascending Colon, Hips, Reproductive Organs, Descending Colon, Lumbar Vertebrae, Adrenal Glands, Bladder, Genitals, Spine.

CHAPTER 10
TIPS FOR REIKI PRACTITIONERS

❝ *Sometimes your joy is the source of your smile, but sometimes your smile can be the source of your joy.* ❞
- **Thich Nhat Hanh**

THE FUNDAMENTALS

There are three fundamental keys each practitioner should learn to develop if they are to reach their full Reiki channelling potential. They are as follows:

- Developing unconditional *'Love and Compassion'* and a true heart felt desire to help and heal others. It is the genuine feeling of love and compassion in the practitioners own Heart that helps to connect with the loving energies of Reiki. Like attracts like and this helps to maximize the flow of Reiki energy through the practitioner and into the client.

- Removing ones *'Ego-Will'* from the treatment and unfounded belief that in some way they are special or superior to that of anyone else. It is not the practitioner that conducts each healing, nor is it the practitioner that determines the results of each treatment. It may be beyond the practitioners understanding as to why a client may be suffering, as every illness and disease has a specific Divine purpose for being there in the first place. It is not the job of the Reiki practitioner to heal any specific ailments. It is their job to connect to the Divine source and allow the spirit and creative-source to perform what is necessary for each individual at any given time. Surrender yourself to the will of the source.

- Non-control and complete surrender to, and trust in, the Divine spiritual energies you are channelling into your client. One must develop an inner belief that what is best for each client will be met and understand that everything has a Divine reason for happening, or not happening as the case may be. Allow your mind & body to be used as a Divine instrument of light by this creative-source and trust in its power. You will be rewarded with deeper insight and increased power for doing so.

YOUR HEART AND YOUR SMILE ARE KEY

Tip: In order to give you a tip, please allow me to first attempt to tell you a joke.

> ❝ *Why do squirrels swim on their backs?*
> *To keep their nuts dry!* ❞

Some of you will not approve of such a joke, however there will be those of you who laughed. However I am not simply trying to be funny. There is a reason for my attempt to humour. Not only is a laugh, or more accurately a smile, contagious and helps to lift the mood of all those around you, science has shown us that by the simple act of smiling, our brains flood our bodies with neuropeptides, serotonin, dopamine and endorphins. This all tells our body and mind to relax and feel happy while helping to lower our heart rate and blood pressure. This prepares our mind and body to be a purer channel for the Reiki energy and helps improve our connection to the Source of Reiki.

Take that energy you felt when you smiled at my joke *(if you did smile of course ☺)*, and during your next healing session, close your eyes, look up and direct that same energy to your whole Heart . This will help intensify your connection to the energy you are channelling because the heart is your key to connecting with the Divine source of Reiki. A genuine heart felt and prolonged smile will do wonders for your health and will improve your Reiki channelling potential exponentially. Just smile to your heart, allow yourself to be open and intend to completely surrender your heart and entire being to the

Divine source. It's through surrendering ourselves to Source that we are guided towards achieving our full potential and our Divine purpose in life.

OPENING YOUR CHAKRAS AND ENERGY FIELD

Tip: Once you are comfortable with the process of giving a Reiki treatment, there is a simple way to open yourself further to increase the flow of Reiki flowing into your body. Try it just before giving your next Reiki treatment.

- **Open your Crown Chakra** – Once you have pepared your space and performed your Gassho and Reiji-ho ritual *(prayer and calling in your guides),* place all 8 fingertips on the top of your head, palms facing to the sides. Now slide your hands and fingers towards the side of your head, bending your wrists backwards as you do so, and opening your fingers until your palms are pointing to the sky. As you do this say, *"I completely open and surrender my Crown Chakra to the Divine Source."* – Now repeat this movement, only this time, pull your fingers and hands towards the back and front of your head, repeating the mantra as you do so.
- **Open your Palm Chakras** – Similar to opening the Crown, touch all your fingers and thumb together on one hand, like you were making a finger puppet. Now point your fingers and thumb towards the palm of your other hand and slowly separate your fingers and thumb until all your fingers are spread out, keeping both palms 4 or 5 inches apart from one another. As you do so say, *"I completely open and surrender my palm Chakra to the Divine Source."* – Now repeat this with your other hand and palm.
- **Open your Crown Chakra again** – Now you have opened your Crown Chakra and the Chakras in both your palms, repeat opening your Crown Chakra one more time with your newly empowered hands.

- **Open your aura** – Now you are ready to further open your complete energy field, or aura. Placing the backs of your 8 fingers together, palms and fingers pointing towards the body, raise your hands to above your head and draw a straight line from above your Crown down the middle of your body. When your hands reach your Root Chakra, your fingers should still be in the same position, with all eight fingers touching and pointing towards your body. Now bend your wrists and twist your arms so that the backs of your fingers are still touching but the tips are now pointing forwards. – Now motion your hands apart like you were doing breast stroke while swimming while saying, *"I completely open and surrender my entire energy field to the Divine Source."* Repeat this swimming motion three times, once at the bottom of your body, once in the middle and one at the top of your head. *(now repeat this on the back of your body, visualizing and intending that you open your energy field completely down the back of your body.)*

By performing this quick and simple exercise you will have opened your Crown Chakra and Palm Chakras further than usual. This will allow for a greater flow of Reiki to enter your Crown and pass through your palms. You can then repeat this process on your clients Crown Chakra and aura before giving them a treatment. Just miss out opening the palm Chakras on your client as you do so, as this is not necessary. This will fully open both you and your client to an increased flow of Reiki energy.

The intention to open your Chakras is what really matters, however it can be helpful to visualize a violet lotus flower on top of your head opening its hundreds of petals as you open your Crown. Similarly, imagine you are opening your palm Chakras as wide as your hand while visualizing your hand turning violet, or bright white, with Divine light as you open each Palm Chakra. Do this quick technique before using Reiki for any purpose and you will be able to channel an increasing flow of energy that grows stronger and stronger with time. You can also use the same technique on all your other Chakras to help open and cleanse them further and faster. Without touching your hands together, open one Palm Chakra first and hold both hands in front of you, palms facing the sky. If your hands are sensitive enough you will be able to feel a massive difference between the Palm Chakra you opened and the one that remains partially closed.

THE IMPORTANCE OF KEEPING YOUR SPINE STRAIGHT

One very important point to remember when channelling Reiki is to keep your spine straight, as your spine affects both your Reiki and your health. All of your vital organs are connected to your spine, so when your spine is misaligned, damaged or you have poor posture, it will contribute towards your overall health. So whether you are an energy channeler or not, ensuring you keep good posture when sitting, walking and lying down is very important for your good health.

The human spine has been held in high regard by our ancient ancestors and is still considered to be sacred by many traditions to this very day. As you are aware, your main energy channel travels down your spine, so when your body posture is poor, it will also have an effect upon the flow of Reiki energy through you and into your client. When one puts a kink in a garden hose for example, the flow of water is restricted and pressure builds within the channel. Similarly, your energy flow will be restricted in much the same way. Good posture involves keeping your head, neck and back straight and the easiest way to achieve this is to stand in front of a wall and lean against it. Your bottom, your shoulders and the back of your head should all be touching the wall while remaining relaxed. When in this position, your spine will be completely straight and the flow of energy through your main energy channel will be improved.

71

PART 2:
REIKI TECHNIQUES

Piglet: "How do you spell love?"
Pooh: "You don't spell it. You feel it." –
Taoism of Winnie The Pooh

CHAPTER 11
THE THREE PILLARS OF REIKI

66 *Look for love and you may find an earthly version of it. Become the embodiment of love and pure love will follow you everywhere.* 99 - **Ricky Mathieson**

The following are traditional Japanese techniques, as taught by Mikao Usui, and are known as the Three Pillars of Reiki. As well as the Reiki Principles, Mikao Usui based his Reiki system on the three pillars, known as: Gassho, Reiji-Ho and Chiryo.

GASSHO MEDITATION – The First Pillar of Reiki

Gassho means *'two hands coming together'* and is the first step taken before giving or sending a Reiki treatment. Dr. Usui called this technique the First Pillar of Reiki and advised his students to practise it twice daily. It is also engraved upon his memorial stone. The First Pillar of Reiki is a special meditation to attune oneself to the spirit of Reiki and should be done as a regular meditation every day. Performing a short Gassho meditation also preceeds the Reiki techniques listed in this book.

Gassho Meditation helps to relax the body, clear the mind and open the heart Chakra, as well as all the other Chakras, and it also strengthens ones ability to channel Reiki. Practising the Gassho Meditation daily will help one to achieve peace and inner stillness and will help develop an awareness of ones inner self. Complete the Gassho Meditation as follows:

Close your eyes and take a minute or two to relax your body and mind. Focus on breathing slowly and deeply. Focus on your breath and breathe in slowly for 5 seconds while being aware of your lungs expanding. When breathing out, exhale for 3 seconds while focusing on your lungs deflating. Keep the palms of your hands together in prayer position with your fingers pointing up and your thumbs touching your heart Chakra at the middle of your chest while performing this exercise.

Now take your attention away from your breathing and focus all of your attention on the tips of your middle fingers. There is an acupuncture point at the tip of the middle fingers called the *'central surge'*, which is activated by this meditation. Your meridians are the energy pathways that interconnect through your body and Chakras. This technique connects the meridian energy channels of the body and best prepares you for channelling Reiki.

If any thoughts arise, acknowledge them and then gently allow them to leave your mind, taking your attention back to focusing upon the point where your middle fingers meet.

As you continue to practise, you will find that you can hold your attention on the middle fingers for a longer period of time without thoughts arising. The longer you can keep your mind free from random thoughts the better.

Keep in mind that it is perfectly normal for thoughts to arise when doing this meditation. Do not feel as though you have failed or are making a mistake. Keeping your head clear of thoughts is no easy task and will take practise. As soon as you realize that you are focusing on a thought, brush it to the side, allow it to gently leave your mind and refocus your attention upon the tip of your middle fingers.

This meditation can be done either standing or sitting, just remember to keep your spine straight while remaining as comfortable as possible. Continue this meditation for around 15 to 30 minutes per session. Once or twice a day if possible.

When you have reached the end of your meditation for that session, take a few deep breaths, bring your attention to your eyes, then slowly open them when you feel ready.

Remember to stand up slowly if in a seated position as you may be light headed after performing the meditation.

There are many individuals who find meditation difficult, either finding their minds constantly wandering or feeling as though they do not have the time of day to practise such a technique. However meditation plays an important part in the on-going development of Reiki. While practising Reiki is important, meditating is equally important to help advance your Reiki capabilities. Through meditation, this helps prepare us to connect with the source of power from which Reiki comes and allows our physical body and mind to increase the strength of this connection.

One of the most powerful attributes to channelling an increasing flow of Reiki is the ability to relax your body and mind while working with the Reiki energy. Although getting as much hands on experience using Reiki and the various symbols is also important, like anything else, it would be best to find a balance between the two. However you will notice a significant improvement in your Reiki channelling abilities if you practise the Gassho Meditation regularly.

If you feel you are struggling to find time to meditate, a good way to create the time is to get up and start your day 30 minutes earlier. This time is for you and it is for your own best interest to find the time to meditate, even if it's only for 10 to 15 minutes a day. Regular meditation will not only improve your concentration and your health, it will help you develop an inner peace and calmness of mind and will greatly enhance your ability to channel an increased flow of Reiki the more you practise it.

When you have reached the point of being able to successfully meditate for an extended period of time and have a solid foundation and practical understanding of how Reiki works, merging the two will offer you much success. When our body is fully relaxed and our mind is clear of thoughts and at peace, we enter a receptive state of being that's best for channelling Reiki.

77

REIJI-HO – The Second Pillar of Reiki

Reiji means *'indication of the spirit'*, or *'guidance of the spirit'*, and Ho means *'technique'*. This is the Second Pillar of Reiki, as taught by Dr. Mikao Usui. It is used to awaken your intuitive ability to discern energetic imbalances in your clients personal body or energy field, also known as the aura. It is the Reiji-ho that prepares the practitioners mind and body before giving a Reiki treatment. To perform the Reiji-ho you can be either standing or seated, then perform as follows:

- Do the Gassho Meditation for a minute or so, with hands in prayer position, in front of your chest with your thumbs touching your heart Chakra. Remember to focus on the tips of your middle fingers and breathing slowly and deeply to help relax your body and mind.
- Ask to keep you both grounded and safe from negative energies and then proceed to say a short prayer on behalf of your client, asking that they be completely healed, for their highest and greatest good.

Now raise your hands, still in prayer position, to your forehead and touch your third eye with your thumbs. At this point, you are asking to be connected with your spirit guides. Whether they be deceased relatives, angels of the light, the spirit of Reiki, Reiki guides, ascended masters, Jesus, Buddha, god, or whichever you prefer. Alternatively, you can intend to connect with the Divine Source, whose power transcends all deities and spirits. Call upon one or as many as you wish. Ask to remain a pure and clear channel to give the spirit of Reiki to your client and for your hands to be guided to where they are needed.

When performing the Gassho Reiji-ho technique, stating your intentions with a pure, clear, open and sincere heart will help improve your connection to the Divine Source and strengthen your Reiki. The Divine Source always knows what hides deep within your heart and Heart Chakra and this is one area students would be encouraged to focus upon developing.

CHIRYO – The Third Pillar of Reiki

Chiryo means *'treatment'* and this is the Third Pillar of Reiki that was taught by Mikao Usui. The original teachings of Dr. Usui did not involve a predetermined set of hand positions, as is practised today. Instead, Dr. Usui encouraged all of his students to rely upon ones inner guidance and to intuitively heal every client using whatever form of guidance came naturally to each student. In this way, each treatment is uniquely focused upon what each client needs to create balance, harmony and well-being within their own body and energy field. Keeping your body in a state of deep relaxation, your mind clear of thoughts and feeling the connection with the energy through your heart will all ensure you remain in the most receptive state, allowing your awareness of guidance to come with greater ease.

When it comes to letting the Spirit of Reiki guide you, everyone will experience guidance in different ways. For some, you may feel your hands being pulled magnetically. You may experience images in your third eye of where your hands should go. You may hear or receive thoughts telling you where to place your hands. You may in time see colours, relating to the colours of each Chakra, as an indication of where your hands should go. Or you may experience none of the above and be able to sense your clients energy field using your hands. For those students who have not yet developed their intuitive skills, it would be advised to perform Reiki treatments using the hand positions that were later added to the system of Reiki by Chijiro Hayashi. This will ensure your client receives a full bodied, balanced treatment.

If you have no sensations or experiences at all when channelling Reiki, do not be concerned. This does not mean that the Reiki energy is not working or flowing. Reiki is activated by your intention to use it, not your ability to sense it. With regular practise, you will become more aware of these subtle energies as your body and hands increase in sensitivity and you become one with the Reiki energy existing around and within you. Until such time, you will find the Reiki hand positions to be helpful.

CHAPTER 12
SMUDGING

66 *Truly love yourself! Love is the blood that flows through your spiritual veins.* 99 - **Ricky Mathieson**

The Sacred Smudging Ceremony is a practice that is thousands of years old and was used by our ancient ancestors as a way of cleansing and purifying an area or space. Still used in Shamanic and other practices today, it is a useful and effective tool for purifying your room before a Reiki treatment. This will clear out negative energies and make your space pure and sacred.

Our ancient Shamanic ancestors have continued this spiritual knowledge forward into modern times and it is said that before one can be healed, or one can heal another, it is beneficial to clear the healer, client and room of all negative energies, negative spirits, and negative thoughts and feelings. This helps to cleanse both our physical body and our spiritual body and improve the spiritual connection between the two. Without cleansing your room before a treatment, healing energies can be diluted when being channelled into each client. This is because the Reiki will automatically gravitate towards any negativity in either the healer, room or client and will cleanse it in the process. Modern day empaths can immediately feel the energy difference in the air after using these herbs and clairvoyants have reported seeing negative entities being driven out of the area after purification of the space using these herbs.

Sage, Sweetgrass, and Cedar are the most common purifiers.

Sage – There are many different types of Sage available, however there are two to use for space purification. The botanical name for *'true'* Sage is *'Salvia Officinalis'*, otherwise known as Garden Sage. Or *'Salvia Apiana'*, otherwise known as White Sage. Salvia comes from the Latin root *'Salvare'*. Meaning *'to heal'*. These two types of Sage are used to cleanse a room, space, or person from negative energies and negative influences and will stop such influences from entering this sacred space once purified.

Cedar – The spirit of the Cedar trees are considered to be very ancient and wise by the ancient tribes. Its botanical name is *'Thuja Occidentalis'*. Similar to Sage, it will cleanse and purify a space in much the same way however it's less smokey.

Sweetgrass – Sweetgrass is a most sacred plant to the Native American Indians. Its botanical name is *'Hierochloe Odorata'*, otherwise known as Holy Grass, or Vanilla Grass. It is said that burning Sweetgrass after burning Sage or Cedar brings in the good spirits and positive influences.

Using any of these natural purifiers, perform The Sacred Smudging Ceremony as follows:

- With a loving pure heart, state a prayer/intention for cleansing and purifying the room or space. An example could be, *"I cleanse this room of all negative energies, negative vibrations and negative entities, and send them towards the light with love and healing blessings"*. Repeat this *'three times'*. Of course you may adapt this to something you better resonate with.
- As you walk around the room, remember to smoke all the corners of the ceiling and any dark places, such as cupboards, to remove all negative energies. Saying your prayer/intention three times as you do so.
- Once you have cleansed your space, smoke your own body to purify your spirit. This is done by simply encompassing yourself and surrounding your body with this sacred smoke.

Please keep in mind that The Sacred Smudging Ceremony is as sacred as Reiki itself and should always be treated with the upmost respect. We are entering into union with the unseen powers of nature, plants, the Earth and the Spirits and there must be honor and respect if the ceremony is to be successful.

CHAPTER 13
STEP-BY-STEP REIKI TREATMENT

66 *You are the author of your lives book. While there may be fixed chapters ahead, you choose how to fill the pages within each one.* 99 - **Ricky Mathieson**

The following instructions explain how to give a Reiki treatment from start to finish and detail each of the many techniques that can be incorporated into every healing session. Follow each of these techniques on a regular basis when giving treatments to yourself or others and you will improve the flow of Reiki during your treatments.

Remember to discuss how a Reiki treatment works with your client and where you will be placing your hands and ask them if they are comfortable with you touching their feet. *(Some people can feel uncomfortable having their feet touched)*

Perform the following:

1. Find a quiet place where you will not be disturbed. Set the atmosphere with dim lights or candles and play soft relaxing music that is free from distracting words.
2. Prepare your space further by burning Sage, Cedar, or Sweetgrass and say a genuine and respectful prayer/intention to clear the room of all negative energies.
3. With your hands in Gassho *(prayer position),* thumbs pointing to your heart Chakra with your focus upon the tips of your two middle fingers, take a moment to relax your body and mind.
4. Perform this simple breathing exercise to help relax: Breathe in for 4 or 5 seconds, slowly and deeply, hold your breath for a second, then exhale slowly for 3 or 4 seconds. Keep your focus on the tips of your middle fingers with your thumbs touching your Heart Chakra.

5. Perform the *'Kenyoku Dry Bathing'* technique on yourself to cleanse your body of any negative energies before treating your client. This can be done at this point or before step 1, or before you begin the whole treatment process.

6. If any thoughts arise, gently sweep them to the side and allow them to leave your head without analysing them. Thinking is natural so do not worry if you do. Just sweep them away. You will improve with practise. When you are breathing slowly and comfortably and are feeling relaxed, perform your Gassho prayer/state your intention. Such as, *"Please keep me grounded and protected from negative energies, negative vibrations and negative entities. Please allow "clients_name" to receive the spirit of Reiki with love and compassion, for their highest and greatest good"*. Change these words slightly to something more appropriate if self-treating.

7. Now that you have set your intention to channel Reiki, keep your hands in Gassho prayer position until you can feel the connection. Otherwise, meditate for a minute or so with your focus still on the tips of your middle fingers.

8. After this, raise your hands from Gassho position, palms still together, to Reiji-Ho *(to your forehead),* and touch your third eye with your thumbs. At this point, you are asking to be connected with your spirit guides. Such as, *"I call upon my spirit guides, my Reiki guides, and angels of the light. Please allow me to be a pure and clear channel to receive the spirit of Reiki with love and compassion"*. Maintain your focus upon the tips of your middle fingers when performing Reiji-Ho.

9. Now proceed to visualize/draw your Reiki symbols. You can draw them into each palm with your middle finger, draw them on your palms with your minds eye, or draw/visualize the Power Symbol on the Chakra of your client. Once you have done this, proceed to place your hands in the first-hand position or use your intuition or Byosen Scanning if you wish *(hand positions and Byosen Scanning are explained later).*

10. You can draw/visualize the Reiki symbols on each Chakra you work on or on any other part of your clients body. There is no limit to how many times you can draw/visualize each symbol, however once you do, clear your mind of thoughts, stay relaxed, and try to feel the connection to the Reiki energy from your Heart Chakra. If you can not feel this connection, don't worry. The energy will still be activated and will work accordingly.

11. Spend five minutes on each hand position. Otherwise move to the next hand position once you feel the energy has decreased or sensation in your palms reduces.

12. Once you have finished with the 8 *(or 12)* hand positions, you will be anywhere between 45-minutes to 1-hour into your clients treatment. You may wish to place your hands upon the arms, shoulders and legs also. Once you have finished this, now place your hands on the soles, or tops, of your clients feet with the intention of grounding them. *(If your client does not want you to touch their feet, place the palms of your hands near the soles or tops of their feet)*

13. State your intention when doing step 12. Such as, *"Please keep "clients_name" grounded and protected from negative energies, negative vibrations and negative entities"*, then spend a few minutes grounding your client.

14. Smoothing out your clients energy field can help balance the energy in each Chakra and can be a pleasurable experience for your client. To do this, simply start at their Crown Chakra and hold your hands a couple inches away from their physical body. Now run the palms of your hands down their middle, from Crown to Root Chakra, and down their legs to their feet. Do this 2 or 3 times with the intention of smoothing the aura.

15. Now you have treated your client, finish by *'Dry Bathing'* yourself to clear any negative energies that may have clung on to your own energy field.

16. Return your hands to *'Reiji-Ho'* position, your thumbs touching your third eye, and thank the guides you called

upon at the start of the treatment. Thank them three times. *(the number three is a sacred number in many religious and spiritual practices)*

17. Finally, return your hands to Gassho prayer position and ask that you remain protected and grounded.

- This concludes your Reiki treatment -

Touch your client on the shoulder and quietly inform them that you have finished your session. Your client may feel light headed and perhaps a little spaced out after a Reiki treatment. So tell your client to relax and take their time getting up. Having your client hold something from the Earth, i.e a stone or crystal, will help to ground them to those grounding energies. Also advise your client to drink sufficient amounts of water for the next 2 or 3 days to flush out any toxins that have been released into their bloodstream as a result of their Reiki treatment. *(Reiki will naturally release the accumulation of toxins within the body into the bloodstream so they can be processed and removed from the body).*

Remember that Reiki uses a light touch, so there is no need to massage your client or to apply any pressure to their body. Make sure you are not leaning on your client during their treatment, which could make them feel uncomfortable. The palms of your hands should be used with your fingers extended and touching together. Not spaced apart. This helps to focus the energy from your palms through to your client.

Remember to drink plenty of water yourself and keep well hydrated. It's also not uncommon to get hungry after you give a Reiki treatment, so you might fancy a snack. With regular channelling, the palms of your hands can become very dry, so it might be a good idea to moisturize your hands after giving a Reiki treatment.

CHAPTER 14
JOSHIN KOKYU-HO – TAN DEN BREATHING EXERCISE

66 *The force of life is in your breath. Breathe well and you shall live well.* 99 - **Ricky Mathieson**

Tan Den Breathing forms an important part of your Reiki treatments and is a technique used to master the flow of Ki energy around your body. With regular practise, this breathing technique will help you to channel increasing amounts of Reiki energy while giving treatments and it's a visualization technique that would be advantageous to use whenever channelling the energy of Reiki.

Below you will see the location of your Seiki Tanden and the main flow of Ki *(or Chi in China)* energy around the upper body.

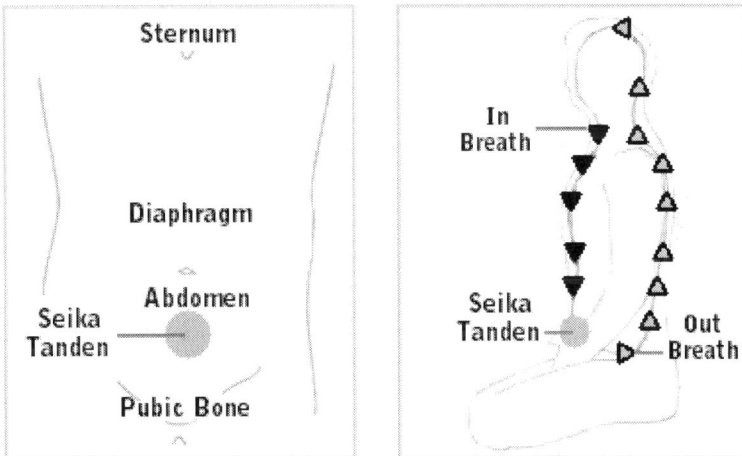

The diagram above on the left shows the point in which your *'Seika Tan Den'* is located, otherwise known as your *'Tan Den'*. This is the point below your naval and mid-way between you belly button and pubic bone. While Ki energy flows through the complete body in a figure of eight, here we focus only on the flow of Ki in the upper body. Perform this technique as follows:

- When breathing in through your nose, visualize white or golden Reiki energy being drawn in from your Crown Chakra, down your front and into your *'Tan Den'*. Touch the tip of your tongue to the roof of your mouth when doing so to connect the energy pathways of your body.
- Visualize your *'Tan Den'* as a ball of white, golden or violet spinning light.
- The bigger and quicker you visualize this ball of light spinning within your *'Tan Den'*, the more Reiki energy will be drawn into your *'Tan Den'* as you inhale.
- Hold your breath for a moment once you have filled your lungs and try to feel the Reiki energy radiate throughout your whole body.
- Upon exhaling through your mouth, drop your tongue from the roof of your mouth, compress your abdomen and imagine the white, golden or violet Reiki energy gently flowing from your *'Tan Den'* up your spine and out through your palms, feet, Chakras, fingers and toes simultaneously. If giving a treatment to a client, the Reiki energy is visualized flowing up the spine to the heart Chakra, then flowing down the arms and out the palm Chakras.

Do not do this technique for more than ten minutes at a time. If you suffer from High Blood Pressure, Asthma, or Heart problems, only do 1 or 2 of these drawing breaths at a time, breathing normally in between, as this technique may increase your Heart rate and blood flow around the body and could increase your rate of breathing if you are not used to the energy.

If you are new to energy work, it would be a wise idea to start slow and gradually build up the amount of energy you draw into our body. This technique can cause some discomfort in your stomach if your body is not used to having such high levels of energy in your *'Tan Den'*. With regular practise, this technique will widen your Meridians and improve the level of healing you are able to offer your clients and yourself by increasing the amount of energy you are able to channel through your body.

CHAPTER 15
BYOSEN SCANNING

❝ *Your energy is contagious. Be responsible for the energy you share. What you share comes back to you.* ❞ **-Ricky Mathieson**

Byosen Scanning, of *'Byosen Reikan-Ho'* as it's known in Japanese, is a technique used to scan someone's energy field with your hands to perceive areas of disharmony or energetic imbalance. Byosen Scanning, which means *'disease line'*, involves using your palm Chakras to feel this imbalance, which signals where the practitioner should place their hands when channelling Reiki. As already mentioned, Mikao Usui encouraged his students to use their intuition and spiritual/inner guidance when giving Reiki treatments and Byosen Scanning is one of the many techniques one can used.

If an imbalance exists within an individual, in the form of mental, emotional, physical or spiritual disharmony, this will always show itself in the energy field around ones physical body as an energy signature of that imbalance. Ensure you are in a receptive healing state in body and mind by keeping yourself relaxed, free from thoughts and try to feel the connection to Reiki from your Heart Chakra. Everyone has varying degrees of sensitivity and some may find Byosen Scanning comes naturally while others need more time and practise before being able to sense someone else's energy field. When your sensing abilities develop further, you may be able to see this energy using your physical eyes or receive other sensory intuitive guidance.

To experiment with feeling another persons energy field, scan your non-dominant palm over the seven main Chakra points *(detailed earlier in this book)*. Keep your palm a few inches above each one so you are not touching the physical body. These are the points of the body where you will be able to sense the energy field the easiest. When using your palms during Byosen Scanning, you could feel any of the following sensations in your palms:

- Heat or cold
- A magnetic like push or pull sensation.
- The sensation of resistance on your palms.
- Tingling in your palms.
- The sensation of pins and needles.
- Feeling as though energy is being drawn from your palm Chakras into your client in a sucking effect.
- Feeling an increase of energy flowing down your arms.

When you feel any of these sensations, this is a sign for where to focus your hands during a Reiki treatment, as this point in your clients body is imbalanced. Once you notice the sensation is your hands decrease, this is a sign that this area of the body has received the amount of energy it needs. At which point it's time to move on to the next Chakra position.

To scan a client, first place your non-dominant hand about ten inches away from their Crown Chakra and keep your attention focused upon the palm of your hand and be aware of the sensation in your palm. Then move your hand to around three inches away from the top of your clients head and begin moving your hand to above your clients forehead. Then proceed to scan down towards their feet. Keep your hand three inches away from their body when doing so at all times. This helps you sense the energy emanating from your clients energy field without skin to skin contact confusing the sensations in your palm. Move your hand very slowly and be conscious of any changes in energy you can feel in your palm.

Of course, there are other forms of intuitive guidance that may not be noticed in your palms. With time and practise you will be able to physically feel the energy fields of your clients. This technique and will also help develop your extra sensory perception the more you work at sensing your clients energy field.

CHAPTER 16
KENYOKU - DRY BATHING

*❝ You are the prisoner, the prison and the prison keeper. Within your heart lies the key to freedom. ❞ - **Ricky Mathieson***

The word Kenyoku means *'dry bathing'* and is a technique for cleansing ones energy field after a Reiki treatment. Dry bathing should be done on yourself after a Reiki treatment to release any negative energy that may have stuck to your aura from the client you are working on. The Kenyoku technique can also be used to cleanse yourself of negative energy at any point in your day, not only following a treatment.

Perform Kenyoku as follows:

- Do the Gassho Meditation for a minute or so and ask to remain grounded and to protect yourself from negative energies, negative entities and negative vibrations.
- Perform Reiji-ho and call in your spirit guides.
- Now place your right palm a few inches from your left shoulder and stroke down your chest across your stomach and end at the right hip.
- Then place your left hand on your right shoulder, stroke down your chest, across your stomach, and end at the left hip.
- Now with your right hand on your left shoulder again, extend your left arm and sweep your right hand down to your fingertips, then fling your right hand out into the air as though you are throwing away any negative energy.
- With your left hand on your right shoulder, do the same.
- Repeat this stroke down your left arm once again, and one more time with your right arm.
- While doing Kenyoku, say a mantra in your head, such as, *"I cleanse my mind, body and energy field of all negative energy."*

- If you wish, you can finish with a short Gassho at the end, thanking the Spirit of Reiki for cleansing your body and energy field of unwanted negative energies.

The Kenyoku Dry Bathing Technique can be done before and after a Reiki treatment or done on its own as a quick energy refresher.

CHAPTER 17
KOKI-HO - HEALING BREATH

❝ *You yourself must strive. The Buddha's only point the way.* **❞**
- Buddha

Koki-ho means *'healing breath technique'* and is a method for directing Reiki using your breath and any of the Reiki symbols you have been attuned to. You may come across a situation where using your hands to give Reiki is inappropriate, such as on clients with burns, small creatures, open wounds, or on areas of the body where having your hands could cause discomfort. Perform Koki-ho as follows:

- Using your intuitive guidance, or using the sensitivity of your palms with Byosen Scanning, locate an area on the client that is in need of healing. Otherwise, focus upon the area you wish to direct your healing breath.
- Breathe in deeply with your stomach and fill your lungs to near capacity. Visualize the Reiki energy flowing down through your crown Chakra and into your 'Tan den', that area deep inside your body mid-way between your belly button and the top of your pubic bone.
- Hold your breath for a moment and visualize a Choku Rei, or any other you wish to use, on the roof of your mouth, and remember to say its mantra three times.
- Now gently and continuously breathe into the area you wish to direct your healing breath and visualize the energy flowing from your Tan Den up your spine and direct it through your breath.
- While you exhale, imagine the symbols you visualized on the roof of your mouth penetrating the area you are blowing the healing breath into.
- You can also use colour when directing energy, such as imagining your breath to be a bright white or golden light. Or if breathing into any of the Chakras, you

can visualize the colour of your breath as the relative colour of whatever Chakra you are exhaling into. Such as imagining your breath to be the colour red when exhaling into the Root Chakra, orange for the Sacral Chakra, yellow for the Solar Plexus Chakra and so on.

- You can perform this technique as many times as you feel is necessary during one treatment.

The Koki-ho can also be used on yourself during self-treatments, or with the Hon Sha Ze Sho Nen Distance Symbol on a photograph of a client or picture of the place you wish to direct Reiki to. As has been mentioned previously, it is the intention to use Reiki that activates its flow. Whether you use your hands, your finger, only your mind or your eyes, the energy of Reiki will flow however you intend it to flow.

You can further empower the Koki-ho healing breath technique by performing it simultaneously with the Joshin Kokyu-ho Tan Den Breathing Exercise. This simply involves completing Joshin Kokyu-ho to draw more energy into your Tan Den and then immediately performing Koki-ho afterwards, intending that the energy stored in your Tan Den travels up your spine and out through your breath.

CHAPTER 18
GYOSHI-HO - HEALING THROUGH THE EYES

66 *You will not be punished for your anger. You will be punished by your anger.* 99 - **Buddha**

Gyoshi-ho is a method for sending Reiki energy to someone, or something, using only the eyes and is a useful technique if you are unable to use your hands for sending Reiki or are too far away to use your healing breath. The technique is as follows:

- Whether you use Byosen Scanning, Reiji-ho, or you simply know where you wish to send Reiki energy, prepare yourself to give a Reiki treatment in the normal fashion. Perform a short Gassho, followed by Reiji-ho and once in a receptive healing state in body and mind, focus your eyes upon the area you wish to send Reiki.
- When you gaze upon the desired area with your open eyes, allow your eyes to be relaxed and de-focused as if your vision was slightly blurred.
- As you do this, try to keep your body relaxed and your mind clear of thoughts. Meditate with your eyes opened, but not focused in a stare, and channel the symbols you intend to use during Gyoshi-ho into the desired area.
- If any thoughts do arise, simply brush them to the side and allow them to float out of your mind without over analysing those thoughts. The same as you would do during the Gassho Meditation or a full reiki treatment.
- Have the lights dimmed or use candles to help soften the strain upon your eyes when performing this technique.
- This can be done for a few minutes or for longer if you feel the need to.

Before beginning Gyoshi-ho, sit opposite your partner for two or three minutes and gaze into each other's eyes. This helps you connect with your partner and allows you both the opportunity to become comfortable and at peace. Staring at another individual can often make them feel self-conscious, so an important aspect of this technique is to relax your partner and make them more open and receptive to the Reiki you are about to be sending them.

Finish this technique by giving thanks to the spirit guides you called upon then ask to remain grounded and protected from all negative energies.

CHAPTER 19
HESO CHIRYO-HO - NAVAL HEALING TECHNIQUE

66 *Your worst enemy can not harm you as much as your own unguarded thoughts.* 99 **- Buddha**

This is a healing technique that can be incorporated into a Reiki treatment or used as a stand-alone practice on its own. Either on a client or on yourself during a selftreatment. Heso Chiryo-Ho is a healing technique that focuses upon healing our energy field via the naval, or belly button, using the middle finger. The naval is considered to be the center of self, the seat of self, or our Seat of Consciousness as it is also commonly known. If using this technique on a client, it would be wise to explain the technique you intend to perform to save any confusement. Perform this technique as follows:

- Perform a short Gassho prayer to enter a receptive healing state in body and mind, ask to remain grounded and protected, state your intentions for doing this technique and call in your guides. If you are incorporating this into a healing treatment and have already done so, simply state your intent before performing this technique.
- Focus on breathing into your *'Tan Den'* while remaining focused upon this area and breathe effortlessly. Connect to the energy of Reiki and try to feel its presence in your heart.
- With your middle finger bent or relaxed, gently insert its tip into the naval, or belly button, using your dominant hand, or your main writing hand. Gently apply a little pressure so that you can feel a pulse. Be aware of this pulse and the Reiki energy and let the energy flow. Try to be in the experience as you do so and merge the Reiki and pulse so you become one with the flow of energy.

- Once you feel the energy decrease, move on to another area of the body. Finish the technique in the normal way by cleansing your own energy field and finish with a short Gassho prayer giving thanks to your spirit guides. Complete your closing ritual by asking to remain grounded and protected from negative energies.

CHAPTER 20
JACKI-KIRI JOKA-HO - NEGATIVE ENERGY CLEANSING

66 *The whole secret of existence is to have no fear. Never fear what will become of you and depend on no one. Only the moment you reject all help are you free.* **- Buddha**

Jacki means *'negative energy'* and Kiri means *'to cut'*. This technique can be used to purify objects and to release and/or transform negative energy from objects, such as rings, jewellery, artefacts, family heirlooms, clocks, stones, crystals or any other object you feel may be harboring negative energies. This can be a useful technique if buying something for yourself or home that is second hand, as you can help to remove any of the energies still attached to it from its previous owner.

WARNING: It is <u>VERY</u> important that you <u>DO NOT</u> use this technique with people, photographs of people, plants, any animal, living species, food or drink.

Due to the energetically harsh nature of this technique, it is commonly taught that it should not be practised unless you are an expert in a certain discipline. Jaki-Kiri Joka Ho is derived from a more potent Japanese spiritual practice known as the *'Ki Barai'*, which is considered something best left to those with a great many years of experience in the *reiryoku no michi* disciplines. For this reason, it would be in your best interest to heed the warning. Cleansing negative energies with this technique is nevertheless simple and very effective. Should you wish to perform this Negative Energy Cleansing Method, please perform the following steps responsibly:

- Enter a receptive healing state in body and mind by doing a short Gassho meditation for a minute or so, with hands in prayer position in front of your chest and your thumbs touching your heart Chakra. Remember to focus on the tips of your middle fingers and breathe slowly and deeply to help relax your body and mind.

- Ask to keep yourself grounded and safe from negative energies then proceed to say a short prayer stating your intention.
- With your hands still in prayer position, raise your hands to your forehead and touch your third eye with your thumbs and ask to be connected with your spirit guides.
- Hold the object in your non-dominant hand *(the hand you do not write with)*. If using this technique on a large object, such as a piece of furniture or a house, stand in front of it so you have the whole house in view.
- Focus on your breathing and be conscious of Reiki pouring in through your crown and flowing down to flood your *'tan den'* with bright white Reiki energy as you do so. Hold your breath for a moment after performing your breathing technique until you can feel the energy accumulate in your *'Tan Den'*.
- Then cut through the air, about two inches above the object, three times with a vigorous chopping motion as you continue to hold your breath. The third cut should stop above the object. The motion of each kiri *(cut)* should be swift and come to an abrupt stop, like you are performing a karate chop.
- Once done, finally channel Reiki into the object until you feel it is fully charged with positive energy.
- This process can also be done at a distance using the Hon Sha Ze Sho Nen Distance Symbol while imagining you are holding the object or are in its presence.

Complete this technique by raising your hands to your forehead in Reiji-ho position once again and thank your spirit guides. Finally, end with a short Gassho and ask to remain grounded and protected from negative energies.

CHAPTER 21
HATSU REI-HO - REIKI SHOWER TECHNIQUE

&& *No matter how hard the past, you can always begin again.*
- **Buddha**

Receiving any Reiki attunement gives one a baseline foundation on which they can build, so while everyone will start upon the same equal footing, how effective your Reiki channelling abilities become depends upon your physical, mental, emotional and spiritual balance. If one has any issues in any of the previous areas, these negative blockages will inhibit your ability to channel increasing levels of Reiki energy. This is why, first and foremost, it is important to focus upon your own self-growth and development, as helping yourself to reach your full potential plays an important part in your ability and effectiveness to help others.

Practising Reiki, deep relaxation and meditation regularly will all help you reach your full potential and the *'Hatsu Rei-Ho'* method is a great practise to incorporate into your daily life. Hatsu Rei-Ho originates from Tendai Buddhism and is used as a purification ritual in many other disciplines. It was only recently, in 1999, that Hiroshi Doi, a member of the Usui's Association, brought this Eastern technique to the Western world. It is a highly effective technique that should ideally be used on a daily basis, regardless of which level of Reiki you are attuned to, for anywhere between 10 to 15 minutes, or longer if you wish.

Hatsu Rei-Ho means *'start up Reiki-technique'* and is an effective way of improving your ability to channel an increased flow of Reiki by increasing the depth, quality and intensity of ones connection to the Reiki energy. You can complete the following technique either sitting on a chair, crossed legged on the floor or standing, and either indoors or outdoors. Just make sure you are comfortable, in a quiet place and will not be disturbed. The following technique has been split into separate parts to help you absorb all the information, however the following techniques should be followed from start to finish as one continuous technique. Detailed steps to perform Hatsu Rei-Ho are as follows:

Sit up straight. Be comfortable, however try to keep your spine perfectly straight, and remain relaxed and peaceful. Rest your hands with your palms down on your knees or legs. Close your eyes and bring your focus to your *'Tan Den'* and simply relax with your mind focused upon your *'Tan Den'*. There is no need to control your breathing. Just relax. Once your breathing has calmed and you feel relaxed, perform the following:

Setting your intention

- With your hands in Gassho position, silently state your intent in your mind. Such as, *"I wish to commence the Hatsu Rei-Ho Reiki Shower and allow the purifying Reiki energies to cleanse my mind, body, aura and soul"*.

Dry Bathing your energy field

- Perform the cleansing *'Dry Bathing technique'*, described on page 91, and sweep any negative energies from your body and arms using the palms of your hands.

Establishing your Reiki connection

- Take your hands from Gassho position and raise them above your head so that your arms are extended straight above your head and separate your palms so that your arms are parallel and shoulder width apart.
- Now bend your hands back at the wrist so that your palms face upwards with fingers pointing out to the side.
- If you wish, you can at this point draw/visualize any or all of the Reiki symbols you have learned above your head or in the palms of your hands.

- In your mind, silently state, *"I am open to the light, I am open to the light, I am open to the light."* Visualize bright white or golden energy flowing down from above into the palms of your hands, down through your arms and spine, and into your *'Tan Den'*.
- When you can feel the energy flowing, slowly lower your hands and place them onto your lap with your palms still facing upwards.

Spirit Cleansing Breath

- Be aware of breathing naturally, however do not focus upon controlling your breathing. Take a moment to relax and just be in the here and now.
- Slowly bring your focus back to your *'Tan Den'* again as you continue to breathe naturally. In your minds eye, visualize and feel the Reiki energy flowing down from above and through your Crown Chakra in a bright white or golden light. Visualize this energy flowing down your body and into your *'Tan Den'*.
- With each natural breath you inhale, imagine yourself drawing more energy in through your Crown Chakra and down to your *'Tan Den'*.
- When your lungs are full and you are about to exhale, be aware of the bright white or golden light growing stronger and brighter and radiating throughout your entire body until it encompasses your surrounding energy field and extends several feet around your physical body. Try to feel the energy as you do so.
- At the moment you exhale, remember to breathe naturally without controlling your breath, be aware that you are emanating this white/golden light from every cell in your body, with the light radiating out in all directions to infinity.
- You may experience various sensations and/or emotions when performing this technique. This is a perfectly normal reaction. Continue this part of the Reiki Shower technique for as long as you feel comfortable.

Giving thanks to your guides

- Once you feel ready to conclude this Reiki Shower treatment, gently bring your hands back to Gassho prayer position, with your thumbs touching your Heart Chakra and your mind focused upon the tips of your middle fingers, and maintain this level of awareness for as long as you wish.
- Once you feel ready to stop, you can thank the spirit guides you called upon at the start of the treatment for being with you while your hands are in Gassho. Alternatively, you can perform another Dry Bathing exercise to smooth out your aura/energy field before returning your hands to Gassho position and giving thanks three times.

Whether you only have 10 to 15 minutes to spare each day on yourself or wish to improve your Reiki significantly, I would recommend this technique as an excellent way to open your Chakras further, improve your connection to the Reiki energy and generally improve your ability to channel an increasing flow of Reiki energy.

CHAPTER 22
PSYCHIC SURGERY

66 *Nothing ever goes away until it teaches us what we need to know.* 99 **- Pema Chodron**

Every one of us has powerful abilities lying dormant inside of us that are waiting for us to activate them. The power to heal ourselves and others is only one of those abilities. All that is necessary is for each of us to awaken that dormant power and work on developing our understanding and ability to use it. Psychic Surgery, also known as Aura Clearing, is a powerful tool that allows one to take charge of their inner power and use it to heal specific issues within themselves and others.

Psychic Surgery is not to be confused with actual surgery, as there are no invasive procedures involved. Psychic Surgery works to heal the body by extracting specific negative energy blockages from our energy field and it's a highly effective and powerful technique for removing energy blocks from specific areas. This includes deeply rooted negative energies that may have accumulated as a result of emotional experiences that remain with us from our past. Your mind, body and energy field are all naturally linked, so what affects you on an energetic level has direct consequences upon your overall health and well-being. Many individuals are not in optimum health because they create blockages within their energy field without even knowing it. This interferes with the natural flow of life energy through the body. Your ideas, beliefs, thoughts, self-talk, emotions and feelings will all contribute towards creating these energy blockages if you do not remain in a positive state of being.

When you create negative blockages within yourself, these blocks lodge themselves in your energy field and affect your body and organs. If these blocks are not removed, they can eventually result in health problems, whether physical, mental or emotional in nature. By removing these energy blockages we clear our energy channels and allow our flow of Ki energy to increase and improve. Psychic Surgery is one technique for releasing these blockages and can be used to treat physical health issues, emotional trauma, mental anguish, addictions, relationship troubles, spiritual imbalances or any other known or unknown root cause of illness or distress.

Cleansing ones aura or energy field using Psychic Surgery can be done as a stand-alone treatment or incorporated into a standard Reiki treatment, whether at the start of that treatment, the end, or somewhere in between. It's a flexible technique that can be used anytime and for any purpose.

The first step is to give the cause of the problem an identity, which allows the Reiki practitioner and client to focus directly on the energy imbalance in question to release the blockage. By giving our problem an identity, we bring the energy imbalance associated with that problem into our conscious awareness, where it can be processed, released and healed.

Perform this technique as follows:

Preparing The Client

1. Ask your client to think about the issue they would like to have healed. It is not necessary for your client to tell you what the personal problem they may have is. It is only necessary that they focus on it during the technique. This is especially important to remind clients as there will be some sensitive issues that many clients would be unwilling to share with you.
2. Ask your client to close their eyes and meditate on their specific issue. When your client is relaxed and you are both in a receptive state to receive Reiki, ask the question, *"If the cause of your problem were to exist in a certain part of your body, what part of your body would that be?"* Remind your client that if they are working on a physical issue, that this issue may be located in an area other than where the physical symptoms are

located. Should your client find it difficult to feel where this blockage might be, tell them to guess what part of their body holds the blockage. There can be no wrong answer. You are only creating a focus for your client.

3. Now ask the client to imagine looking into the area on their body they have chosen and ask the question. *"If the cause of your problem had a shape, what shape would that be?"* This is to help your client visualize the shape of the negative energy blockage that is causing, or representing, their problem. The shape your client visualizes could be a circle, a square, a cube, a pyramid, a mist, a small or large dot, or anything else. The actual shape is not important and there is no wrong answer. Your clients ability to focus their attention on the energetic root behind their specific issue is what is important. Having your client visualize their negative energy blockage and taking part in their own healing can be a very empowering gift for your client. Involving your client and having them participate in their own healing will give the impression that they are directly dealing with the issue themselves. Also keep in mind that there could be multiple locations of negative energy blockages on your client with multiple shapes. If this is the case, have your client tell you which areas are most pronounced and work on these areas first.

4. Now ask the question, *"If this shape had a colour, what colour would that be?"* Then ask, *"If this shape had a texture, what would that texture be?"* Slippery, jagged, rough, bumpy, smooth, or anything else. Then ask, *"How heavy is this shape, how much does it weigh?"* Then ask, *"Is this shape hot or cold?"* Then ask, *"If this shape made a sound, what sound would it make?"* Remember, the answers are not important, neither is your clients ability to answer all the questions. What is created for your client is a point of focus for them to be consciously aware of while using as many of their senses as possible to identify with the root cause of their energy blockage. Having a location, shape, colour,

texture, weight, temperature and sound for the root cause allows the person to be connected to the nonintellectual, energetic attributes associated with their issue. This gives them the ability to observe the behaviour of the shape while you perform Psychic Surgery on that blocked area.

5. Help empower your client by asking them if they are willing to release their issue and be completely healed from it. Ask them to continue focusing upon the shape and to be willing to let it go. Your client should acknowledge any impressions or thoughts they may become aware of when this negative energy blockage is released. This is the lesson they are to learn.

The Process

6. Remember when performing this treatment that your client can be seated, lying on a therapy bed, or standing. The position of their body is not important.

7. Draw/visualize your Usui Master Symbol, Dai Ko Myo, in the palm of both your hands and repeat the Mantra, Dai Ko Myo, three times as you do so. Now do the same with Choku Rei in each palm. Draw a large Choku Rei down the front of your body for protection. Then draw small Choku Rei's over each of your seven main Chakras to empower them.

8. Now extend your Reiki fingers. This is done by grabbing hold of your fingers with one hand and imagining the hand you hold is made of stretchy rubber which you can stretch out to between 12 and 18 inches in length. Once you have done this, draw one Choku Rei at the ends of your extended fingers and without touching your hands, brush them over your palms to feel their presence. (*Do this with both hands.*) Try to feel your extended fingers and the power they contain as you move them around.

9. Psychic Surgery is done with your full attention and focus, using your physical, emotional, mental and spiritual selves. It should be done with complete

confidence in your own ability and your trust and reliance in the power of Reiki.

10. Say a prayer, either out loud or to yourself, and ask the creative-source, your Reiki guides or angels of the light etc., to work with you to create the most powerful healing possible. Ask that the healing take place with Divine love, compassion and wisdom so that the highest good of your client may be served.

11. Ask the client where the cause is located in the body and what its shape, colour, temperature, weight, texture, sound, etc. is. Ask them to focus on the area and be willing to let go of the shape and be healed. Draw/visualize Choku Rei over the area where the block is located.

12. Stand in a powerful and confident position and using the full strength of your total being, imagine you are reaching into your clients body and grabbing the negative energy with your extended Reiki energy fingers. Then pull it out and send it up to the creative-source. Do this with physical, emotional, mental and spiritual intention and using the full strength of your being. You may be able to see, feel, or sense the negative shape being released from your client, however this is not necessary to perform Psychic Surgery successfully. If you can feel this negative shape or are aware of it somehow, use this perception to guide it out your client and release it.

13. When you pull the negative energy out from your client, breathe in with your lips partly opened. When using your breath to exhale, breathe out and imagine you are breathing the negative energy up to the creative-source. When doing so, imagine you are breathing this negative energy into your hands, stopping it at your wrists and allowing it to go no further, preventing you from pulling the negative energy into yourself.

14. Do this process as many times as you feel is necessary, reaching into your clients body, pulling the negative

shape out with your intended Psychic fingers and releasing it to the light.

15. After a minute or so, ask your client how they feel, asking, *"what does the shape look like now?"* As you heal your client the shape may get smaller or change in colour, texture, weight, temperature, etc. These are all signs the process is working.

16. Should the shape not change in some way, or remains after you perform Psychic Surgery, try pulling at the blockage from a different angle, or different side of your clients body.

17. Continue to perform Psychic Surgery on the blockage, periodically asking your client what the shape looks like now. Eventually, the shape will disappear completely. When this happens, ask your client to carefully look inside themselves to be sure the blockage has completely gone and to see if anything that doesn't belong remains inside. Such as fragments of the shape or something that doesn't belong there. Continue performing Psychic Surgery until the shape has completely gone from your client, while your client continues to inform you of their on-going progress.

18. Once the shape is gone from your client, draw/visualize the Choku Rei Power Symbol over the area and give it Reiki to fill the area with light and complete the healing. Now step back and make a karate chop in the air between you and the client to break any psychic cords that may have been formed. Also remember to retract your extended Psychic Reiki fingers by pushing them back into your physical fingers.

What do we need to know?

Most negative energy blockages can easily be removed using this technique. If not, then it is likely that the cause of the blockage has a message for the client before it will release. There may be a lesson your client needs to learn and it may be necessary for them to interact consciously with the root cause of their negative blockage for it to release and heal completely.

If this is the case, perform the following:

1. Draw Sei Heki over the area and continue to send Reiki to this area. As you do, ask your client to silently talk to the cause to let it know that they respect the information it has to offer and that they are ready to hear what it has to say. Ask it to tell you what it needs to do in order to heal. Then ask your client to focus on its shape, telling you whatever comes into their mind. Even if this seems like nonsense. You can also use this opportunity to mention any intuitive information you become aware of yourself. Ask if any of the information that comes to you makes sense to your client. You may be able to help your client by connecting your intuitions to the root of their problem. There may be deep rooted feelings of guilt, anger, hatred, or jealousy for instance, that your client needs to let go of in order to heal completely. However, allow your client to decide what feels right and what makes sense with the emotions that come up and allow them to heal themselves without being suggestive. This is an important point when performing this technique to help empower your clients own healing.

2. Once you have an idea for what the client needs to let go of, ask them if they would now be willing to do so. If yes, continue to focus doing Reiki on the area and ask your client to focus their attention on the shape and to let go of the anger, jealousy, guilt etc. they have attached to that shape while doing so. Releasing the shape from their body and allowing it to heal with forgiveness. The client can then let you know when they feel ready to move on.

3. When the client is ready to move on, ask them to focus upon that area to ensure the shape is gone. If it's still there, continue to perform more Psychic Surgery. The experiences your clients may have had and the abilities

of the healer will vary. So some people may take more time or sessions in order to facilitate a deeper and more complete healing.

4. Once done, always finish by using a Choku Rei Power Symbol over the area with the shape, filling it with Reiki and healing light. Then perform a karate chop to rid any negative energy cords between you. Remember to retract your psychic fingers once you have concluded the technique and perform a Kenyoku Dry Bathing on yourself at the end to clear away any residual negative energy that may have clung to your energy field.

Performing a one-hour Reiki treatment after performing Psychic Surgery can be especially helpful for your client to completely heal. Some issues have more than one level, so your client may find that once an issue has been released, it may cause further issues to surface that were hidden underneath. Doing more Psychic Surgery on these deeper areas in the same fashion as before can help your client heal each additional layer of negative energy that may surface.

Keep in mind, your client could also experience any physical symptoms as they go through this healing process. Or what is commonly called a healing crisis by many. This could be experienced either during the treatment or sometime after. Reminding your client of this is important to avoid any misunderstanding or confusion.

Inform your client to drink sufficient amounts of water, to eat healthy and to reduce their intake of alcohol, caffeine and sugar and to sufficiently rest for the next two or three days. This will be beneficial for your client as this all helps aid the healing process by limiting the amount of unhealthy substances within their body. This will ensure the Reiki you channel into your client will work for their maximum benefit without the energy becoming diluted as a result of having to cleanse any impurities present within their body.

CHAPTER 23
CREATING A REIKI GRID

❝ *Observation without evaluation is the highest form of intelligence.* ❞ - **Jiddu Krishnamurti**

Keeping an open mind, trying new techniques and experimenting with Reiki will help you understand Reiki better and connect with it on a deeper level. To improve your healing abilities, it is a good idea to venture into the unknown to see what works best for you. The Reiki crystal grid is quick and easy to set up and can be used to send Reiki to anyone or anything on a continuous basis. Remember, your only limitation with Reiki is the limitation you place upon your own imagination. If you intend for Reiki to work, it will follow your intention. Just like channelling Reiki into a person, intending for Reiki to flow into a Crystal, for instance, needs only your intention to be successful.

The crystals you should use for your Reiki grid should be quartz crystals and you will need eight of them in total. Quartz crystals have unique properties which allow them to absorb and hold thoughts and intentions as well as other energies. Due to this, you are able to charge quartz crystals with your intentions *and* your healing Reiki energy. This allows the crystal grid to continue to send energies to wherever you desire when you are busy doing other things. Programming your Reiki grid to send healing Reiki energies to yourself, other people, goals, desires, the planet, or anything else you wish to achieve, is simple and effective and the crystals you use play an important role.

CHOOSING YOUR QUARTZ CRYSTALS

- Choosing the best quartz crystals for your Reiki Grid are important and you should rely upon your intuition when making your selection of crystals. To select your crystals, you can either use a pendulum over the crystal,

Byosen Scan each one to sense the energy coming from each Crystal, choosing whatever crystals draw your attention or any other form of intuition, select the 6 Crystals which will make the outside ring of your grid. Generally, these crystals can be raw and rough or rounded and smooth. The choice is yours.

- Now select the crystal that will take its place in the center of your crystal grid. Choosing crystal quartz for this again, you can use a crystal skull, a crystal ball, a crystal pyramid, or a raw cluster of crystal quartz.
- Your master crystal needs to be a long crystal. This is the Yang or male type energy crystal and is used for bridging the energies of the other 7 crystals on your grid together.

CLEANSING & CHARGING YOUR QUARTZ CRYSTALS

Before placing your crystals on your Reiki grid, you will need to cleanse them of any negative energy they may be holding.

There are a number of ways to do this:

- You can place all eight crystals in a bowl of pure salt water and channel Reiki over the bowl, intending for all the crystals to be cleansed and blessed for sending distance Reiki using a Reiki grid.
- You can cleanse your crystal under cold running water, intending that each crystal be cleansed of all negative energies.
- You can place your crystals outside touching the Earth while remaining in direct sunlight, or direct moonlight for a day. Intend that the sun or moon removes all negative energies from the crystals.
- Using White Sage, Cedar, or Sweetgrass, perform a short prayer/state your intention, and smudge your eight crystals using the smoke to cleanse them.
- Alternatively, you can do none of these and cleanse your crystals using only Reiki and intention.

Once you have selected your quartz crystals and cleansed them of any negative energies, it will be necessary to charge each crystal with positive energy and intention. To do this:

- Hold your eight Reiki crystals in your hands, or place them on a floor or table between your palms, and draw/visualize the Distance Symbol over them all. Take a minute or so to charge the crystals with Hon Sha Ze Sho Nen. This allows you to send Distance Reiki through the grid towards your future desire.
- Continue the process until you have charged all eight crystals with the Reiki symbols you've been attuned to.

Now you are ready to create your Reiki Crystal grid.

SETTING UP & CHARGING YOUR REIKI GRID

The picture below shows an example of a Reiki Grid arranged upon one of the four Tibetan Antahkarana symbols.

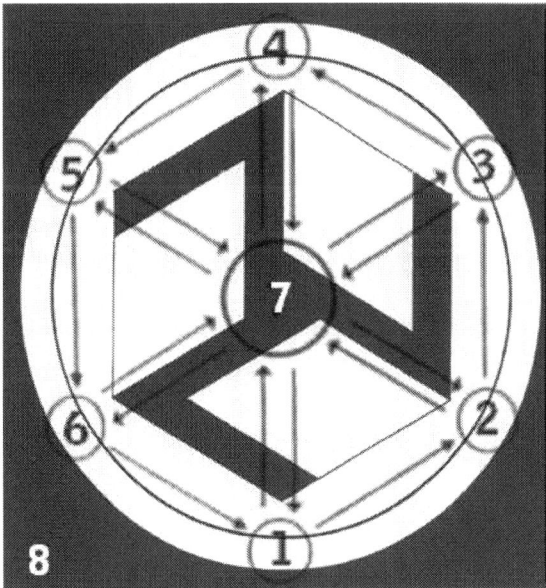

Once you have completed the previous steps it is now time to set-up your Reiki Grid. You can print the antahkarana on paper or buy professional cotton prints from the internet. If you plan on moving your Reiki grid, put your antahkarana and grid upon a stiff piece of cardboard or wood so moving it is easier.

To create your Reiki Grid, perform the following:

- Take your crystal ball, skull, cluster, or pyramid of quartz and place your main crystal in the center of the Reiki grid. Use either the Female or Male Antahkarana, depending on your intentions.
- Now place each of the six crystals around the central crystal. Position all six crystals pointing towards the central crystal if you're using straight edged crystals.
- The master crystal is kept off the Reiki grid, as shown by position number 8.
- Now place a picture of yourself under the central crystal with a positive affirmation written on the back. For example, you could write your goals, desires or your version of the Reiki principles on it. Then place the central crystal on top of this to send Reiki to yourself.

To charge the complete Reiki Grid, perform the following:

- Each day, spend 15 to 20 minutes charging your Reiki grid by laying your hands upon the central crystal and channelling the Reiki symbols you have been attuned to into it. You should use all the Reiki symbols available.
- Now use your master quartz crystal to bridge the energies from the central crystal, to the other six crystals. As you link your complete Reiki grid with your master crystal, do so as directed by the arrows on the grid illustration. Like you were cutting a piece of cake. Do so either clockwise or anti-clockwise, whichever you feel more drawn to. Move it from crystal number 1 to the center crystal (7) and back. Then bridge to the next outer crystal, to the center, then back again. Continue

till you have bridged all six crystals with the central crystal. When doing so, repeat a continuous series of affirmations, such as, *"I charge this Reiki grid with love, with love, with love, with light, with light, with light, to heal, to heal, to heal."* OR *"I connect this Reiki grid to my illuminated spiritual guides, to heal, to heal, to heal."* Or decide on a variation or affirmation you prefer.

- Continue using the Master crystal to bridge the entire circle of six crystals to each other and the central crystal. Repeat this a further two times, so three times in total. Continue to repeat your affirmation each time.

Now your Reiki grid is prepared and ready to go. As your picture containing your personal affirmation will be under the central crystal, Reiki energy will continuously be directed towards you and your written desires. All you have to do to send Reiki from your grid to another person, desire or intention, is to add a piece of paper containing that persons name and desire and place it under the main central crystal.

Charge your central crystal every day for 15-20 minutes to ensure healing energies are continuously being directed towards the Reiki grids intentions. When your goal has come to pass, or when you feel it's time to remove any of the names from your Reiki grid, make the intuitive decision to do so.

ABSENT CHARGING YOUR REIKI GRID

If you are away from your Reiki grid and not able to get your hands on it to charge it each day, remember that you can also charge it from a distance once attuned to Reiki level II. Take a photograph of your Reiki grid and carry it with you when travelling and take your master crystal with you. The other seven crystals stay on your Reiki grid.

Using the Distance Healing Symbol, *Hon Sha Ze Sho Nen*, connect with your Reiki grid using your picture of it. Using your master crystal, you can then bridge the crystals by tracing your master crystal over the picture of your grid. Remember to include your intentions under the Reiki grid and repeat your affirmation when doing so.

The energy of Reiki works by preparing and focusing the mind and the heart. Therefore carrying a picture of your Reiki grid to distance charge it will eventually not be necessary once you have learned to automatically channel the energy at will. The goal of Reiki is to teach you the relationship between energy, your body and your mind. Once you have this deeper understanding of how energy flows with thought and how this energy is reinforced by your emotions, you will become increasingly aware of how to channel Reiki by will alone, without the need for symbols or detailed visualization exercises.

In truth, it is your complete being that creates your reality and how you experience the world depends upon your perception and awareness. Understand this through direct experience and you will realize how your thoughts and emotions determine the experiences you attract into your life. When you further reinforce the attractable energy of your thoughts and emotions with the Divine energy of Reiki, directing the future events of your life will soon become second nature. Your beliefs can either limit or improve your ability to use your mind productively and efficiency when channelling energy of any type.

CHAPTER 24
PSYCHIC PROTECTION TECHNIQUES

❝ *Thousands of candles can be lit from a single candle and the life of the candle will not be shortened. Happiness never decreases by being shared.* ❞ **- Buddha**

Completing the second degree Reiki attunement not only gives you more tools and capabilities for using Reiki on yourself and others, it also further opens your connection to the Source. The higher the Reiki degrees you complete, the more your mind and body opens to these refined spiritual energies.

Cleansing yourself of negative energies on a regular basis with Reiki is an important part of the practice, whether you have completed only the first level attunement or higher degrees. However, as the higher degrees improve your spiritual connection and increase your sensitivity further, it becomes increasingly important to protect yourself from the negative energies that are all around you. If you find yourself advancing to Reiki Master Teacher level, psychic protection should be an especially important part of your practice as you will be increasing your psychic abilities and connection to the spiritual world. Protecting yourself at any level is simple, quick and highly effective and there are a number of options for doing so.

REIKI PROTECTION – Creating An Energy Shield

We have all no doubt been in the position when we have felt our energy being sucked out from us and it's an unhealthy, as much as it's an unpleasant, experience. As mentioned earlier, in the chapter on the Choku Rei power symbol, you can visualize/draw this symbol surrounding every side of your body, all six sides as though you were standing in a cube. By setting your intention to *"Protect me from unwanted negative energies",* you can successfully shield yourself from energy vampires and those who may be absorbing your energy unknowingly. Perform this technique as follows:

- Do a short Gassho meditation and prayer, asking Reiki to *"Protect me from unwanted negative energies"*.
- Once you are in a receptive healing state in body and mind, begin your visualizations.
- Now draw/visualize a Choku Rei on each of the six sides surrounding your body.
- Colour can add an additional element to your healing sessions and likewise, can be used to protect one from psychic attack. When drawing each Choku Rei, visualize them in the colour indigo, the colour associated with psychic protection. Alternatively, you can also imagine them to be Divine bright white light that emanates all around you.

This is a handy technique for using Reiki to guard yourself from negative energies and influences. For more serious intrusions, the following Psychic Protection Technique is especially powerful.

PROTECTIVE ANGELIC ENERGY CIRCLE – Divine Help

This is not a technique commonly taught in Reiki, however it is so powerful and effective that I feel it would be advantageous to include it in this guidebook should you ever feel the need to use it. Not only can it block unwanted negative energies, it can also be used to remove negative entities that may be attached to your energy field. Perform as follows:

- Find a quiet place to sit where you will not be disturbed.
- Sit crossed legged on the floor, or in a chair, and close your eyes.
- Relax your body and mind and enter into a receptive healing state.

PSYCHIC PROTECTION TECHNIQUES

- Place your hands in Gassho position and say a short prayer and ask to remain grounded and safe from negative energies.
- Visualizing a Choku Rei Power Symbol, draw a circle of bright golden light around the floor with it, completely surrounding your body. This circle should be in the appearance of a bright, constantly moving ring of energy. In the image of moving golden electricity that flows continuously in a circle on the floor around your body. Alternatively, use white or the colour indigo.
- Now imagine this golden electrical like energy circle completely cocooning yourself in a bubble, all around you, above you and below you, extending several feet.
- Stay inside this circle/bubble for the duration of this technique and do not leave it until you have finished.
- Then with your hands still in Gassho position, repeat the following, *"I call upon the Divine protector, Archangel Michael, to remove all negative energies and negative entities from my mind, body, aura and spirit and to fill my complete being with love and Divine protective light".* Repeat this three times with intention.
- Within this bubble of protective light, visualize filling the inside of it with bright indigo coloured light.
- Now state, *"I intend that all negative energies and negative entities be removed from this circle/bubble of light and my mind, body, aura and spirit and that only love and light are permitted to enter".* This can be said three or more times in a mantra like fashion.
- You may be able to feel the change in energy and a sudden sensation of peace come over you. You may also physically feel any negative entity that has attached itself to your aura be sucked out from inside you.
- When you feel you have successfully completed this technique, say a short prayer. Remember to keep your hands in Gassho position for the duration of the process.

In my experience, this is an extremely powerful and effective technique for removing negative entities that may have attached themselves to your energy field. As a word of warning, you should not conduct this technique without using the universal energy of Reiki and Archangel Michael. This visualization technique can be done without using either, however you will be using your own personal energy field if you do so. Once depleted, you will feel mentally and physically drained and will be more susceptible to negative psychic influences.

Remember, the most powerful Reiki comes from the heart. When you call upon the Archangel Michael, the Divine protector of the heavenly realm, with a pure, loving or even fearful heart, he will respond to your needs.

DEVELOPING YOUR PSYCHIC ABILITIES

We are all psychic to some degree, whether we notice this or not, and we can choose to either develop our psychic awareness or block it. Being attuned to Reiki can sometimes automatically awaken ones psychic abilities, however we can speed this process along by channelling Reiki with the intention to open our Third Eye Chakra to develop our psychic abilities.

Our psychic abilities can be improved with Reiki and this is an area one would be encouraged to develop further. When we improve our psychic awareness and intuitive skills, the guidance that follows becomes easier to recognize. However one should balance their on-going spiritual development between pursuits of the mind and pursuits of the heart until they reach the point of using the heart only to channel Reiki. We can use the Reiki symbols to improve our psychic connection and expand our awareness by channelling energy into our Third Eye Chakra with the intention of opening it. This Chakra is known as the seat of our intuition and source of inspired thought and you can perform this technique as follows:

1. Enter a relaxed healing state in body and mind.

2. Visualize Choku Rei and Sei Heki upon your two palms or visualize them on your Third Eye Chakra.
3. Now place one palm on your Third Eye Chakra *(on your forehead)* and the other directly opposite on the back of your head.
4. Set your intention that Reiki should cleanse and heal your Third Eye Chakra to awaken its psychic abilities for your highest and greatest good.
5. Now simply channel Reiki to your Third Eye Chakra for 10 to 15 minutes.

Performing Reiki on your Third Eye will help to cleanse and heal your pineal gland, which is your doorway to increasing your psychic ability and extrasensory awareness. Performing this technique for extended periods of time may cause some people to experience mild headaches, because the energy is healing a part of your brain that is seldom used during every day waking consciousness. If you do experience headaches when performing this technique, take a break and practise at a later time. Also remember to drink sufficient amounts of water to keep yourself well hydrated, as your body will naturally use up its storage of water when channelling Reiki.

CHAPTER 25
REIKI MEDITATION - CONNECTING TO THE SOURCE – (A)

❝ Meditation brings wisdom. Lack of meditation leaves ignorance. Know well what leads you forward and what holds you back and choose the path that leads to wisdom. ❞ - **Buddha**

Meditation plays an important part in developing your Reiki abilities and this will help you reach your full potential. This Reiki Meditation is best done every day and in the morning if possible. However any time of day or night will do fine.

The Reiki Meditation detailed below, not to be confused with the Dai Ko Myo Moving Meditation, is very powerful and effective and combines the physical and psychological benefits of meditation with the spiritual healing power of Reiki.

Practising this Reiki Meditation on a regular basis will help improve relaxation, mental clarity, creative visualizations, clairvoyant abilities and healing skills and will help develop ones level of consciousness and awareness. If you have a specific problem you wish solved, the Reiki Meditation can help manifest a solution. Likewise, if you have a goal you wish to achieve, using this Reiki Meditation will help surround you with the most productive energies possible. Find a quiet place where you will not be disturbed and perform the Reiki Meditation as follows:

1. Sit in a comfortable position, place your hands anywhere and inhale deeply and slowly with your eyes closed until you have entered a relaxed healing state.
2. Directly in front of you, visualize a large *'Dai Ko Myo'* symbol, or draw one using your fire finger *(your middle finger on your dominant hand), and* visualize the symbol as bright white or violet light as you do so.
3. Repeat the *'Dai Ko Myo Mantra'* three times while focusing upon this symbol. Take a few minutes or so to

connect to it and feel its energy increase. If your mind wanders, gently regain focus on the Dai Ko Myo symbol and continue to focus upon it for up to ten minutes.

4. Once you have spent up to ten minutes meditating on the Dai Ko Myo symbol, imagine the symbol floating up towards the ceiling, through a brilliant white membrane that covers the ceiling in a plain of light. See the symbols popping through this membrane as though it were a bubble containing Divine white light.

5. Now bring your attention to back in front of your eyes.

6. Repeat steps 2-5, this time using the *Choku Rei* Power Symbol, the *Sei Heki* Mental/Emotional Symbol and the *Hon Sha Ze Sho Nen* Distance Symbol.

7. Once you have performed this with each of the Usui Reiki Symbols, you will be more centered within your own power and charged with the creative energies of each Reiki symbol. *(Now you are ready to proceed to the second part of the Reiki Meditation, Manifesting Your Desires.)*

MANIFESTING YOUR DESIRES – (B)

Now you have prepared your body, mind and Reiki, it's time to work towards manifesting your goals and desires.

Complete the Reiki Meditation as follows:

State your goal out loud or mentally, and create a picture of it in your minds eye. Imagine your goal sits in front of you and you have already achieved it. Spend a few minutes focusing upon your goal in front of you with a thought and feeling of accomplishment at having already achieved it. This is an important part of the technique and this is also a fundamental principle of the Universal Law of Attraction. It is our expectation of a future outcome that helps create our belief in that future manifestation coming to pass.

8. Once you have meditated on the image of your goal, the visualization of which could be written in text or in an image, state, *"If this goal is for my highest and greatest good, with Divine love and wisdom, so let it be."*

9. Now send your goal up through the brilliant white membrane of light, just as you did with your Reiki Symbols. Imagine the Reiki symbols surrounding your goal in a cube like fashion with their energies beaming towards your goal.

10. To finish the Reiki Meditation, place the tip of your tongue to the roof of your mouth and focus upon your *Tan Den*, located just below your belly button.

11. Now visualize/draw the Choku Rei Power Symbol in front of your body, with its spiral around the area just below your naval and repeat the Choku Rei Mantra three times. Hold your attention on your *Tan Den* for up to ten minutes, or longer if you wish. This will help to release any excess of energy that may have built up in your head by moving it down to your Seat of Consciousness in your *Tan Den*.

12. Continue to breathe deeply and slowly while focusing on your *Tan Den*. When you are finished, take a few big deep breaths, slowly open your eyes and bring your awareness back into the room.

IMPORTANT: You need to trust that your goal has been established and will come to pass in time. Completely let go of any further thought or deliberation upon that goal. As previously mentioned and to emphasize the point, this plays an important part in the *Universal Law of Attraction*. You send the energy out to your goal, *(The Reiki Meditation process)* and you then draw the goal back in *(trusting it will happen then releasing it from your conscious attention)*. Therefore our belief is paramount. Little can be achieved of any great significance without first having belief.

CHAPTER 26
DAI KO MYO - MOVING MEDITATION

66 *Your vision will become clear only when you look into your heart. Who looks outside dreams. Who looks inside, awakens.* 99
– **Carl Jung**

The moving meditation involves entering a deeply relaxed state of mind while performing slow movements with your arms and hands and its effects can be noticed instantly. If we are to achieve our goals, being in a resourceful state of mind and body is desirable and the Moving Meditation can help us maintain that harmony when we may feel out-of-balance.

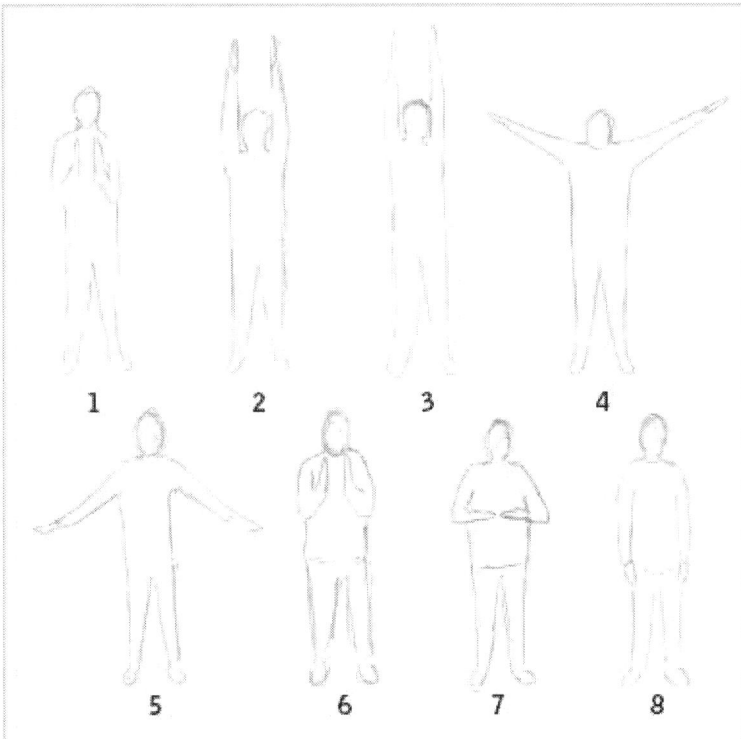

Moving Meditation Arm Movements

If you are attending a meeting, giving a presentation, making a speech, or simply planning on being around a lot of people, this technique will help you release any negative feelings you may have created and attached to that event and will replace them with strong and positive energies. This will help you to feel energized and confident and will bring in the energies you need to help you create a more desirable state of being.

Being able to consciously influence ones mind is a powerful technique for developing the self and improving ones connection with Reiki. One of the most powerful ways to influence your state of mind is through moving the body. Your mind and body have a direct connection with one another and what affects one affects the other. Your thoughts and feelings create chemical reactions throughout your brain and body and help to influence your mood and energy levels. However your posture also directly affects your state of mind by emitting subtle energies depending upon how you position your body. So you can appreciate how one could go round in negative circles if they forget that their mind and body are interconnected. By moving our body in a positive and empowering way, we can emit healthy positive energies from our body that can positively alter our state-of-mind and being. Dancing, playing, exercise and posture can all be deeply healing when used in such a way.

The Dai Ko Myo Moving Meditation is similar to a Qi Gong or Tai Chi exercise and helps to integrate the Reiki energy more directly into the physical body and aura. This creates a strong connection with the Earth and helps to heal the lower Chakras as a result. Incorporating Reiki energy with healing Mantras and positive movement is a powerful and effective combination and this technique helps you become clear, focused and more centered in your own power. Everyone has a unique life purpose, however everyone's purpose should be to re-discover their spiritual consciousness and inner self. This is our true nature and this technique helps us discover that. Remember your 'Heart Chakra' and being more connected to your Heart and smile when performing this exercise. The Heart holds 'love and compassion' and developing your heart is the key to receiving Divine blessings. Reiki is a first step towards achieving that goal.

Perform this technique as follows:
The physical movement:

1. Stand with your feet shoulder width apart, relax your body and enter a healing state of mind.
2. Draw/visualize any of the Reiki symbols you have learned into the palms of your hands. Use all of them if you wish, however including the higher level *'Reiki Master Symbol'* is always advantageous.
3. Now face your palms together, fingers pointed forward and 6 inches in front of your Heart. Keep your palms about 6 inches apart from one another.
4. Keep your body relaxed and your mind clear and connect with Reiki. Meditate on the energy flowing between your palms as the energy builds in strength. You may feel sensations of tingling in and around your hands, a very low vibration, or simply be aware of the change of energy around you.
5. Stay in this moment for a few minutes and let the strength of Reiki build. Now move your hands straight over your head, your palms still facing one another.
6. Then turn your palms so they face out to each side.
7. Slowly lower your arms round in a circle until your palms are horizontal with the ground.
8. Continue this circle until your palms are facing one another, 8 inches apart, with your fingers pointing down to the ground. Keeping your palms facing one another, continue to raise your hands back up to where you started from, in front of your Heart Chakra.
9. As you bring your hands back up in front of your Heart, take a slow deep breath. Then when you breathe out, turn your palms to face the floor and motion your hands downwards towards your feet and Earth and imagine sending the energy down through your legs

and feet and deep into the Earth's core. Visualize that you can actually see this energy going deep down into the Earth and be open to feeling the energy flow return to you from the Earth in a green light.

10. Remember to do this exercise with a feeling of confidence, power and belief and to smile sweetly.

The Mantra:

1. As you continue to repeat the previous physical movements, chant the sacred Mantra of the Master Symbol, *'Dai Ko Myo'*, either out loud or in your head once you begin to raise your hands from your hips. Start the Mantra as you move your hands upwards and end it as they come back in front of your heart. Then motion the energy downwards into the Earth.
2. Repeat this entire process *'three times'*.

Chant:

1. Now repeat the whole previous process, however this time, substitute a new chant while doing your physical movement. Say, *"I establish my Divine presence on Earth"*, doing so slowly and confidently.
2. Repeat this three times.
3. Now do the entire process using the sacred Mantra, *'Dai Ko Myo'*, doing this three times, just as you did the first time.
4. Then do the entire process again using the following chant, *"I accomplish my Divine purpose on Earth"*. Repeating this three times.
5. Now do the entire process again, using the sacred Mantra, *'Dai Ko Myo'*, doing this three times, just as you did the first time.

This completes one set of the Dai Ko Myo Moving Meditation. Do as many sets as you feel necessary. Doing this exercise at any time, even in a spare 5 minutes, will help to open your Crown Chakra to Reiki while keeping yourself grounded with the mother energies of the Earth by connecting you to the Earth's core.

This helps improve both your connection to the Earth, your connection to Source and your energy levels. Performing the Reiki Moving Meditation before giving a Reiki-treatment or teaching a class will better prepare your energy. Or you can do it any time you feel the need for more confidence, self-belief and personal power.

With continued practise, you will be able to receive an increasing degree of energy which can be used to help achieve an instant resourceful state of being and mind. The level of energy one can create using this technique is very powerful. This can be a good technique to complete before any of the other techniques in order to open your energy bodies to their full current channelling capacity.

CHAPTER 27
HUI-YIN - UNDERSTANDING ENERGY FLOW

66 *There is nothing more dreadful than the habit of doubt. Doubt separates people. It is a poison that disintegrates friendships and breaks up pleasant relations. It is a thorn that irritates and hurts; it is a sword that kills.* 99 **– Buddha**

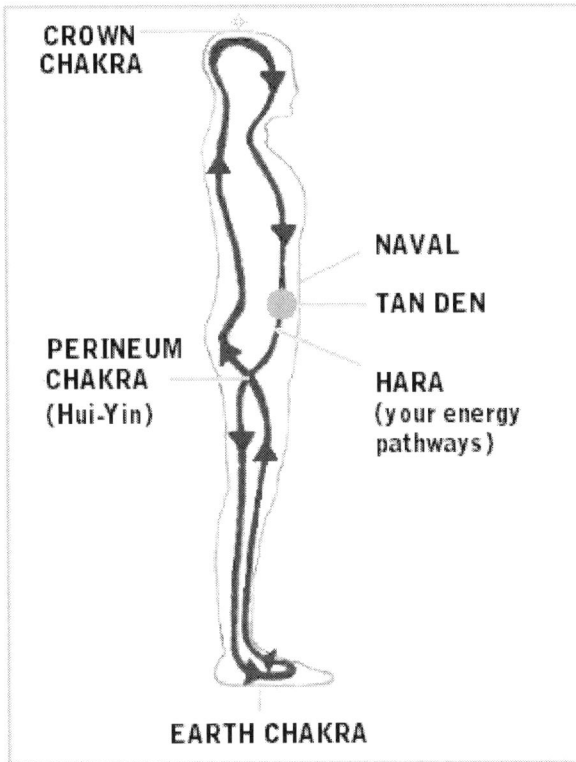

CROWN CHAKRA

NAVAL

TAN DEN

PERINEUM CHAKRA (Hui-Yin)

HARA (your energy pathways)

EARTH CHAKRA

Understanding the energy channels of the body and how Reiki enters and moves through them plays an important part in increasing your abilities as a healer. It is also a necessary technique one should master if planning on teaching others as the Hui Yin plays a vital part in being able to pass attunements to your students.

By learning to control the flow of Reiki energy through your body, you will learn to draw a greater flow of Reiki, store it in the body momentarily and then transmit this accumulation of energy from your body to another. Doing this technique is simple, however it may take a little time training the muscles of your body before learning to use it effectively.

The previous figure shows how Ki energy moves through your main energy pathways and around your body. Your Hara, or Hara Line as it is also called, is shown in this diagram and the arrows represent the flow of energy in through the Crown Chakra, down the front of the body, crossing over towards the back at the Hui-Yin point, flowing down the back of the legs, along the soles of the feet, back up the front of the legs, crossing over at the Hui-Yin point again, and continuing up the spine towards the head. This is how the natural flow of energy flows through your body. However this energy also flows through all connected energy pathways towards your palms and everywhere else in the body.

It is being able to consciously manipulate the flow of Ki energy and holding that energy within your body that enables a Reiki Master Teacher to transmit Reiki attunements.

CONNECTING YOUR ENERGY PATHWAYS

Connect your pathways with the following two steps:

STEP 1: First connect the channels at the bottom *(Root Chakra)* of the body by contracting your Perineum, or your Hui-Yin.

Please be aware that contracting the Hui-Yin is slightly different for men and women. The Hui-Yin point is located at the Perineum, shown on the following figure if you are a male. To contract this point, draw the muscles of the Anus up and in.

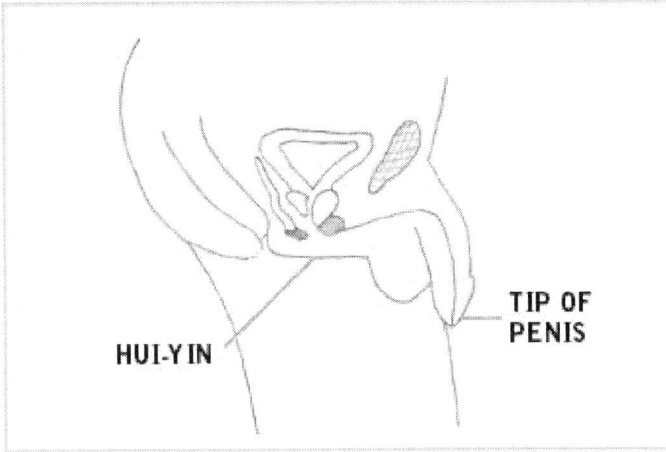

Male Hui-Yin Point

If you are female, you have to contract the anus, as if you were trying to draw your rectum up into your body, and contract your vaginal muscles, as if trying to stop the flow of urine.

If you are familiar with Kegal exercises, those performed after child birth to help stimulate orgasms or control the bladder, you will be familiar with this technique. This connects your lower energy pathways. Please see the following diagram:

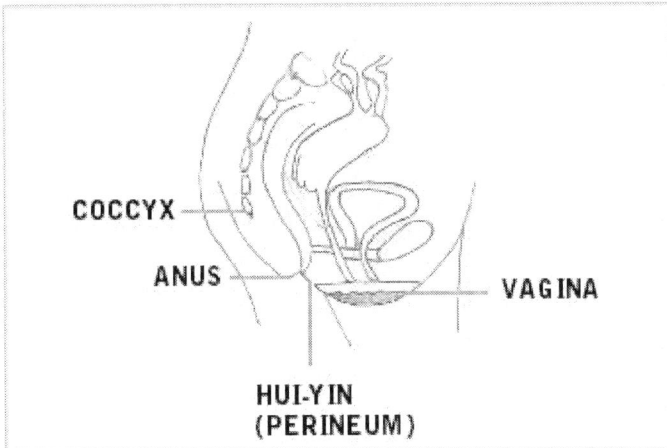

Female Hui Yin Point

Perform the second step as follows:

STEP 2: Second, connect the channels at the top of the body by placing the tip of your tongue upon the roof of your mouth, in the groove just behind your top front teeth.

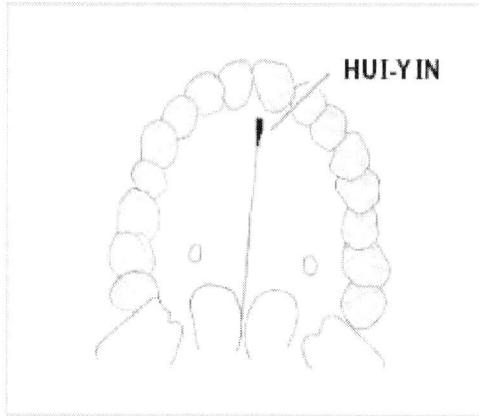

HUI-YIN

Being able to contract and hold both your Hui-Yin points for a couple of minutes, while breathing normally, will be necessary if you are to learn how to pass Reiki attunements to other people. This is something you should start doing now to build enough strength in your muscles if you plan on passing attunements. Practising once or twice a day would be recommended until you can hold your Hui-Yin for at least 3 or 4 minutes at a time.

WHAT HAPPENS WHEN YOU CONNECT THESE PATHWAYS

When we connect our lower energy pathways, Ki energy immediately begins to move upwards in the body, up the spine and along the Hara. At this point, the energy can no longer move downwards to leave the body through the feet and internal organs. A connection is also made to the Earths energy, which too is drawn upwards into the Hara.

When we touch the tip of our tongue to the roof of our

mouth too, we then close the complete energy circuit of our body. This now allows Ki energy to flow from the Crown downwards, as well as from the Earth upwards while holding this energy within ourselves in a repeating flow or loop around the body. This is the process necessary to activate your Hara and you will soon learn to feel this energy flowing around the body in a figure of eight fashion, as described at the start of this section.

PLEASE NOTE: By performing this exercise, you are closing your Root Chakra. Remember to release it frequently if performing this technique for extended periods of time, as not doing so can result in a degree of temporary discomfort. Take it slow, build up your awareness of the energy inside of you, how it feels, how it flows and how it works. Try to feel your energy become one with the energy of Reiki and reach for it using your whole Heart. Your key to limitless potential rests within your Heart.

CHAPTER 28
REIKI MASTER MEDITATION

❝ *It is better to conquer yourself than to win a thousand battles. Then the victory is yours. It can not be taken from you, not by angels or by demons, heaven or hell.* ❞ **– Buddha**

The Reiki Master Meditation involves using the Hui-Yin technique, as described in the previous chapter, and is different from the Moving Meditation and the Reiki Meditation. The *'Reiki Master Meditation'* is a meditation commonly used in Qi Gong, which involves circulating energy throughout your Hara energy circuit and seven major Chakras. Performing this technique regularly will fully open and clear your seven Chakras, your Hara pathways and will remove blockages and heal the body as it does so. This all helps maximize the volume of flow you are able to channel during your Reiki sessions and the benefits are quick and significant.

With regular practise the Reiki Master Meditation will open your mind and body to higher frequencies of energy. What you have learned so far is only the start of your journey and encouraging you to continue in your spiritual exploration and development would always be advised. After all, re-discovering our true self and our spiritual nature is the collective purpose of all our lives. This meditation will help cleanse you of negative energy, purify your mind and body and release any negative energy trapped in your Chakras automatically as you circulate your Ki around your Hara. Be seated or sit comfortably, perform your starting ritual to enter a healing state in body and mind and then proceed with the technique.

Perform this technique as follows:

Begin by first connecting your energy pathways. Contract your anus/vagina and touch the tip of your tongue to the roof of your mouth to interconnect your Hara, as explained previously.

- Put your hands in Gassho prayer position with your third eye focused upon the tips of the middle fingers, and say a prayer and give thanks for the energies you are being sent.
- Draw/visualize Dai Ko Myo, the Usui and Tibetan Master symbol if you have been attuned to both, on each of your palms. Place your palms on your legs or knees and intend for Reiki to flow for the duration of the meditation.
- Visualize a Choku Rei over the front of your Solar Plexus Chakra and keep your hands on your knees or legs and hold that image there for up to five minutes.

Now repeat with Choku Rei on the Sacral Chakra. Then the Root Chakra. Then back up the spine to the Sacral Chakra again. The Solar Plexus Chakra. The Heart Chakra. The Throat Chakra. The Crown Chakra, The Third Eye Chakra, The Throat then the Heart Chakra at the front of the body.

Include the following during your visualizations:

- When performing the previous technique, visualize a sphere of shining bright white light inside each of the Chakras as you visualize each Choku Rei passing over them. Visualizing this energy ball to be spinning can also draw more energy into your channel.
- When you are just about finished, continue to visualize this ball of white light travelling round your Hara pathways, in a figure of eight, and intend for the energy to continue to do so after you have finished your meditation.

You can now release your Hui-Yin and relax your tongue.

If you have made it to this level of Reiki, this is one technique you should practise daily. Not only will it improve your physical, mental, and emotional health, it will also improve your spiritual connection and increase the rate of flow of your Reiki. After practising this technique daily for a couple of weeks, you will notice a significant improvement in your channelling abilities.

The desired frequency of practising each technique in this book is mentioned throughout, however practising *every* technique *every* day is simply not practical. Through your own trials you will become aware of what techniques serve you best. However becoming familiar with how the energy of Reiki flows through your body is important. This helps you become aware of how the energy flow within your body works in tandem with the energy flowing through your Crown chakra from the Source of Reiki. This will help you properly understand the relationship between your own energy and how it interacts with Divine energy.

Doing this technique regularly will also help prepare you for passing attunements, as you will be working on strengthening the necessary muscles in your body to pass those attunements every time you contract your root Hui-Yin point.

CHAPTER 29
REIJU EMPOWERMENT

66 *In the end, only three things matter: how much you loved, how gently you lived, and how gracefully you let go of things not meant for you.* 99 **– Buddha**

The following technique is known as the Reiju Empowerment and is split into two parts. Part one describes the necessary preparations one must make before giving a Reiju Empowerment. Once you have prepared your mind and body, part two describes exactly how to pass a Reiju Empowerment to another person.

Preparation before giving the empowerment

- Stand in front of your client and place both hands on your Tan Den, which is an inch below your belly button. Place your non-dominant hand over your dominant hand with your fingers pointing downwards.
- Connect to the Reiki energy, draw this energy into your Tan Den, pause once your lungs are filled and upon your exhale, expand this energy field from your Tan Den to fill your entire aura and the room. This connects you to the client and makes the space sacred.
- Now raise your hands straight up in the air above your head, palms pointing upwards, with the intention of connecting to Reiki.
- Feel the energy flowing in through your palms, down your arms and body and into your Tan Den.
- Now bring your hands slowly out to the sides and lower your arms towards your hips with your palms still facing upwards. As you do so, imagine you are bringing bright white or golden energy in through your Crown Chakra, flooding energy over your body and aura, and passing this energy through your body into your Tan Den.

- Finish this movement by hovering your hands over your Tan Den, with your dominant hand closest to your body and your non-dominant hand hovering a few inches over that hand. *(Each of our seven main Chakras have energy centers that rest 4 to 6 inches in front of each chakra)*

This technique expands your energy circle and engulfs the room and client with Reiki energy. This will clear the room, make the space sacred and connect you to your client. Once you have performed the slow sweeping arm movement, you have surrounded yourself with Reiki energy and brought it into your Tan Den. Hold this position until you feel a real sense of connection with the Reiki energy. This is one movement and needs only be done *once*. We now follow this movement with *three* repeated movements.

- With your hands still hovering over your Tan Den, move your hands away from you, straight out in front, palms facing forward. Move your hands upwards to above your head to achieve the same connecting position as before.
- Now bring your hands slowly out to the sides, just as before, only this time imagine that as you do so, you are expanding your energy to engulf the person you will be empowering. Return your hands to the Tan Den once again, just as before.
- Now repeat this energy expanding sequence two more times. Each time finish with your hands hovering over your Tan Den.

Giving a Reiju Empowerment

Now you are prepared to give a Reiju Empowerment, touch your client on the shoulder to indicate that they should hold their hands in Gassho prayer position, your eyes closed and body and mind relaxed. Now proceed to perform the following steps:

- You should still be standing in front of your client at this point.

146

- Move your hands high above you with your fingers spread and feel the energy flowing down into your palms from above.
- Once the energy is felt, move your palms closer and join together both index fingers, each finger pad touching the other. Your other fingers should be relaxed and floppy.
- In one continuous movement, move your hands downwards in front of the client and draw down a line of light, which enters the Crown Chakra and draws a line down the center of their body *(with the intention of opening their Chakras)*. Continue to slowly lower your pointed index fingers until you are pointing at your clients Root Chakra.
- Continuing this one movement, part your hands and with your palms facing down, move your hands sideways past the knees and down to the floor, intending to ground your client as you do so. Move your hands to the sides as you stand up straight again.

Now you are going to be holding a number of hand positions that flood four of the major Chakras with healing Reiki energy. Each hand position should be held for at least 30 seconds, however you can extend this to a longer treatment if you wish.

Crown Chakra – Stand up from ritually grounding your client and move your hands down so they are hovering, one hand above the other, a few inches directly above your clients Crown Chakra. Hover your hands over the top of your client, not touching their head but touching their aura instead, and keep your non-dominant hand hovering over your dominant hand with both palms faced down. Now direct the energy from their head, down the energy path you visualized down the center of their body *(do so with intention only, keeping your hands hovering above your clients Crown Chakra without moving them).*

Temples – Following the outline of the aura, a foot or so away from your clients physical body, move your hands to either side of your clients head. Each palm facing each side of the clients head, in line with their eyebrows, so your hands hover a few inches from their temples.

Third Eye Chakra – Follow the outline of your clients aura and move your hands to the front of your clients forehead and make a triangle with your index fingers and tips of your thumbs. Keep all other fingers spread out. *(This is said to represent the symbol of the sun, or life force)* Hold the center of the triangle in the center of your clients third eye. Your palms facing their forehead and imagining a bright stream of white light shining through the triangle in your hands and into your clients third eye.

Throat Chakra – Hold one of your hands behind your clients throat area and the other in front, with the intention of flooding the throat with light.

Heart Chakra – Hold one of your hands behind your clients heart area and the other in front, with the intention of flooding the heart with light.

Hands – Now touch together the fingertips of your first three fingers, as if in prayer position, and move your hands down and over your clients hands, without touching them. Let the energy flow through your clients hands and flood the hands with light.

Once you have finished flooding your clients hands with Reiki, move your hands *(from the three fingertips touching position)* down towards your clients knees. Smoothly and slowly separate your fingertips and with your palms faced down, move your hands sideways past the knees and curve them round in a circle towards the floor. *(Do so with the intention of scooping up any excess energy and returning it to the source of Reiki by bringing your hands together, little fingers touching one another at their tips, with palms faced upwards and the sides of your hands touching one another, as if scooping up a drink of water from a river.)*

Move your hands upwards pointing your fingers towards the center of your clients body, as if you were scooping up the energy and returning it to The Source in the sky. Return the excess energy upwards along the energy pathway you created down the center of your clients body, from your clients Crown to Root Chakra. As your hands reach towards the sky, open your hands out and round to bring your hands back into Gassho, ready to close your session.

- This completes the Reiju Empowerment. -

CHAPTER 30
ADVANCED GROUNDING TECHNIQUE

66 *Eyes are useless when the mind is blind and the heart is closed. You don't need eyes to see, you need vision.* 99 – **Ricky Mathieson**

Grounding your clients following their Reiki treatment plays an important part in their healing. However as a healer, ensuring you keep yourself grounded is also of prime importance. Grounding yourself on a regular basis should be a priority and there are many books on the subject of healing that don't give grounding the attention it deserves.

Keeping yourself grounded helps provide a bridge between the spiritual world and the Earthly plain and helps to create balance in our physical and emotional state of being. When one is not grounded to the energies of the Earth, common symptoms such as dizziness, sensitivity to noise and light, increased negative emotions and feelings of being spaced out, among many others, could all be potentially experienced.

Science has proven that the surface of the Earth is negatively charged, or in other words, contains more negative electrons than positive protons. When an individual's bare foot touches the Earth, whether on sand, rock, soil or grass, an automatic balancing occurs. Science has documented that the highly sensitive nerve endings on the soles of our feet, interact with the negative charge of the Earth. If the human body contains too many electrons, the Earth will automatically absorb any excess electrons from the body through the soles of the feet. Similarly, if the body contains too little electrons, the Earth will automatically provide the body with additional electrons. This helps to create balance and equilibrium within the physical body of every human being. All one needs to do is to stand barefoot and make direct contact with the Earth for this automatic and natural process to complete. So even if you are not a Reiki practitioner or energy worker, you can still improve your health by connecting to nature through the soles of your feet. This has been proven scientifically. For those who are energy workers, ensuring you remain grounded becomes increasingly important the further one advances with their energy work. Because of the importance of grounding ourselves, all energy workers would be advised to keep themselves grounded on a daily basis. Not just at the end of a Reiki treatment. Whether energy channelling or not, grounding ourselves is vital for our good health.

Grounding yourself can be done using the previous natural process. Alternatively, one can complete this next exercise. The following advanced grounding technique, as is documented in the publication *'Reiki Tummo – An Effective Technique For Health and Happiness'*, is shared with you here with the permission of Master Yogi, Irmansyah Effendi, to which I extend my thanks. Please feel free to share this technique with others.

Perform this technique as follows:

- Locate a quiet room where you will not be disturbed during practice. Dim the light so that you can be more relaxed. If possible, you can play music with nature sounds such as running water, or you can play New Age music. You can also burn incense or use essential oils made especially for assisting relaxation.
- Sit down and relax either on a chair or on the floor (with a rug or mat).
- Make sure your spine is straight without forcing yourself. If you sit on a chair, try not to lean on it. If this is difficult, you may lean on the chair, as long as your back is straight.
- Close your eyes so that you can focus your attention easier.
- Place your hands on your lap palms up in a receiving position.

- Inhale deeply without forcing yourself. Exhale and feel that all the tension in your body is breathed out with your exhalation.
- Inhale deeply and do so naturally without forcing yourself. Exhale and feel that your body becomes very relaxed.
- Inhale deeply one more time without forcing yourself. Exhale and feel that your body and mind become very relaxed.
- Now you can start the grounding technique. Focus your attention on your crown chakra. Feel the Divine light in the form of bright white light coming down and touching your crown chakra. The crown chakra becomes more active, turning to the left and to the right while cleansing itself. More Divine light flows to the crown chakra. The crown chakra becomes cleaner and blossoms like a bright lotus.
- The Divine light penetrates the crown chakra at the center and enters the head. It fills up the top, the middle, and then the lower part of the head. From now on, the Divine light flows through the crown chakra continuously becoming brighter and stronger with time.
- The Divine light will erode all impurities from your head and push them out of the third eye chakra.
- More Divine light flows in from above and the light coming out of the third eye chakra becomes cleaner with time. The third eye chakra rotates to the left and to the right, cleansing itself and becoming more active. Let the light flow for some time until the third eye chakra cleanses even more.
- The Divine light flowing into the crown chakra increases. While some of the light still flows from the third eye chakra to expand the third eye chakra further, the rest of the light within the head starts to flow down into the throat. While flowing into the throat, the light erodes all the impurities and negative energy in the throat and drags them out. After the throat is full of light, all

impurities and negative energies are pushed out through the throat chakra at the center of the throat.

- Let the Divine light flow out through the throat chakra until it becomes cleaner with time. The throat chakra rotates to the left and to the right to become cleaner, more active, and more expanded.

- The Divine light flows down increasingly and starts to enter the top portion of the chest. Some of the Divine light enters the left shoulder, the right shoulder, the upper left arm, the upper right arm, the lower left arm, the lower right arm and the fingertips. The Divine light continues to flow, filling up both arms and dragging all impurities from the arms. All tension at the nape of the neck erodes and is dragged out by the Divine light. All the impurities and negative energies are dragged out by the Divine light through the right and left palm chakras and the chakras at the fingertips.

- The Divine light fills up the upper part of the chest and then flows down to fill the chest up to the diaphragm. All impurities in the cells and body organs in the chest are eroded by the light and dragged out through the heart chakra at the center of the chest. Let the Divine light flow out of the heart chakra and drag out all the impurities in the chest. The chest becomes cleaner with time. The heart chakra rotates to the left and to the right to become cleaner, more active, and more expanded.

- For those who have problems with their heart, lungs, or respiratory system, imagine the Divine light eroding away all the greyish unclean energy in the problem area. The greyish impure energy is dragged out by the light through the heart chakra and through nearby pores of the skin. Have the intention to make the particular body part with problems become cleaner and brighter until finally all greyish unclean energy is totally gone and replaced with bright Divine light.

- The Divine light flows through the crown chakra stronger and stronger. While still flowing out the third eye chakra, throat chakra, and heart chakra to make all these chakras more developed, some of the Divine light starts to flow down through the diaphragm and into the upper abdomen. The Divine light fills up the upper abdomen and cleanses all cells and body organs in the upper abdomen. The Divine light drags out all impurities from the upper abdomen. The Divine light drags out the impurities from the upper abdomen. This area gets cleaner with time. The naval chakra rotates to the left and to the right and becomes cleaner, more active, and more expanded.

- Now, while flowing from the third eye, throat, heart, and naval chakras, the Divine light starts to flow down into the lower abdomen. The Divine light fills up the lower abdomen, erodes all impurities and negative energy, and drags them out through the sacral chakra located at the pelvic bone. Let the Divine light flow out through the sacral chakra dragging out all the impurities from the lower abdomen. The sacral chakra rotates to the left and to the right to become cleaner, more active and more developed.

- The Divine light from the head flows down into the neck bone, cleansing the neck bone vertebrae by vertebrae while flowing down and dragging all impurities. The Divine light keeps flowing until it then reaches the spine. The Divine light also cleanses the backbone disc by disc until it reaches the tailbone, and also cleanses the tailbone vertebrae by vertebrae. After reaching the lower end of the tailbone, the Divine light flows out through the base chakra located at the end of the tailbone, dragging out all the impurities with it. Let the Divine light flow out through the base chakra until all impurities are totally dragged out. The base chakra rotates to the left and to the right to become cleaner, more active, and more developed.

- While flowing in through the crown chakra and flowing out through the other six major chakras, the Divine light also flows toward the hips, filling the hips. It then flows and fills the thighs, cleansing as it flows. The Divine light then flows toward the knees, ankles and heels, cleansing these body parts as well. The Divine energy finally flows out through the chakras at the arches of the feet and the smaller chakras at the tips of the toes, dragging all impurities out.

- Relax and feel how clean and bright our body is now. The Divine light flows continuously through the crown chakra to cleanse the whole body and all the major chakras. At the same time, Divine light flows out through the major chakras, and through the palm chakras, the fingertip chakras, and through the chakras at the arches of the feet and the tips of the toes, cleansing your major chakras and your whole body. If you have health problems, focus your attention on the body part with problems. Have the intention that all grey energy in the body part is eroded and cleansed by the Divine light, and dragged out through nearby pores of the skin. The body portion with problems becomes cleaner and brighter with time. Feel the body portion becoming clean and healthy.

- Now, if you are sitting on the floor, allow the Divine light to flow out though your base chakra to flow down towards the core of the Earth. If you are sitting on a chair with your feet on the floor, let the Divine light flow through the arches of your feet and down towards the Earth's core. The energy flowing out of your body touches the floor, penetrates the Earth, layer by layer, and flows down further until it reaches the core of the Earth.

- Channel your love and all positive things to the Earth's core. Let the Earth return your love with a bright green light.

- While letting the Divine light flow into the Earth continuously, feel the bright green light from the Earth start to flow up from the Earths surface. The bright green light flows up like a cylinder that is the size of your body. The energy reaches your lower body and climbs further. It reaches your buttocks, waist, solar plexus, chest, neck, cheeks, and the top of your head and climbs further. After reaching a height of about 3 feet *(1 meter)* above your head, the bright green light starts to open like an umbrella to form the top portion of a giant egg that will give you protection.

- The bright green light flows continuously from the Earth upwards though your body. The top portion of the giant egg flows down further and reaches the height of your head at a distance of about 3 feet *(1meter)* around your body. The top portion of the egg extends downwards further, reaching the height of your face, neck, chest, solar plexus, abdomen, waist, buttocks, and down further until it reaches the floor. Finally, the giant egg closes at about 3 feet *(1 meter)* below your body. The giant egg is now completely formed and it will give you protection.

- As soon as the green egg is formed, the bright light that flows through your crown chakra only flows to your heart chakra. The bright green light from the Earth also flows up only to the heart chakra. At the heart chakra, the two lights mix and then flow in all directions through your whole body, giving positive things to your life and your health.

- Now, have the intention that although you stop practising this exercise, both energies will keep flowing continuously.

- Move your fingers and open your eyes with a smile.

- This completes the grounding technique –

As this technique is rather long, you may find it easier to record a voice clip of the previous advanced grounding exercise. Anyone can perform this technique using the power of their mind through creative visualization. If you have already opened your heart, channel from the heart with no visualizations. We are all spiritual beings having an Earthly experience, so keeping oneself grounded to the physical world plays an important part in our spiritual development, as well as improving our health.

PART 3:

THE REIKI SYMBOLS

"Do not dwell in the past, do not dream of the future, concentrate the mind on the present moment." **– Buddha**

CHAPTER 31
JAPANESE KANJI WRITING SYSTEM

❝ *Happiness does not depend on what you have or who you are. It solely relies on what you think.* **❞ – Buddha**

The Japanese writing written below is known as the Japanese Kanji, a Chinese system of writing adopted in Japan in the 4th Century A.D. Each one depicts the word, *'Reiki'*. However the Japanese Kanji offer a far deeper insight into the word *'Reiki'* and its associated meaning. The word Reiki, as written in Kanji, is written in two Kanji. The top part being one Kanji (translating to *'Rei'* – meaning *'spiritual'* or *'sacred'*), and the bottom being the second Kanji (translating to *'Ki'* – meaning *'energy'* or *'life force'*). This is the traditional meaning of the original Kanji for Reiki.

靈氣　靈氕　靈気　靈氕
1　　　2　　　3　　　4

1. **Kaisho Old Standard Style** – This is the original standard style of writing for how Reiki was drawn during Dr. Mikao Usui's lifetime and pre-world war II.
2. **Sosho Modern Cursive Style** – This version is a simplified shorthand style which writes quicker.
3. **Kaisho Modern Standard Style** – This style is similar to the printed style of Kanji which is taught in Japanese schools.
4. **Gyosho Modern Semi Cursive Style** – This is a simplification of the standard style, allowing it to be written in a faster, more flowing fashion.

Kanji are Chinese symbols used in the Japanese language and consist of characters that represent a certain meaning that corresponds to a word, or group of words. When the original Kanji, the traditional version used by Dr. Usui and before his time, are perceived in its entirety, the original Kanji for the word *'Reiki'* can be seen to hold a deep encoded message within its design.

WHAT IS KANJI

The Reiki Kanji is a symbol in itself and its origins can be traced back to ancient times. The Reiki Kanji symbol is powerful and holds deep significant meaning. The original is a symbol that can be meditated upon as well as used for personal protection and to aid in the development of your own personal growth. The original Reiki Kanji is regarded to be a very sacred symbol that was kept secret by the Reiki Masters and practitioners of the ancient world because of its deep coded meaning and the power it connects with. Symbols are gateways to energy and the Kanji, much like the Reiki treatment symbols, hold great power and understanding for those able to decipher their meaning.

It is said that the Reiki Kanji can be used to balance the energy radiating from any person, object or feeling, and that if placed within a room or on a wall within a picture frame for instance, that the energy associated with it can protect that room and keep it safe. Certainly the original Reiki Masters of the ancient world were well aware of its meaning and power and went to great lengths to keep its pictography secret from those uninitiated into the Reiki secret society.

In the Western world we have come to know the word *'Reiki'* as meaning, *'Universal Life Force Energy'*. If we take the original Japanese Kanji however, the Kaisho Old Standard Style which was used during Dr. Usui's time and before, we can see there is far deep meaning associated with these characters and the word *'Reiki'*. The translation of the original Japanese Kanji for *'Reiki'* holds the following deep and significant meaning.

THE HIDDEN MEANING OF THE REIKI KANJI

Looking at the Kanji for the word *'Reiki'* on the next page, you can see the literal translation for each of the characters. The original Kanji was changed in appearance several times. What can be said for certain is that, the modern Kanji version does translate to the word *'Reiki'* however, its deeper meaning and the energy associated with the symbol are both slightly different in nature.

Looking deeper into the Kanji characters for *'Reiki',* we get a more complete understanding of the symbol. An interpretation of the first part of the original meaning associated with the Reiki Kanji is as follows: *"REI..."*

- The Reiki Kanji reveals the relationship between humanity and Reiki. It is a picture which shows the union between our own energy, *'Ki'*, and the spiritually guided Divine energy of the creative-source, *'Rei'*.
- The fine *"veil between Heaven and Earth"* above falls to *"Earth"* in the form of *"raindrops"*. The ancients relied on rainfall for agriculture and drinking water, a substance that signifies the very source of life itself which was considered to be a blessing from the universe, heaven, or the gods.
- The gift from the universe, the gods, or from *"heaven"*, falls from a shower of *"rain drops"* (the source of life) and into the *"body/container"*, which is representative of the human body.

The imagery of this part of the Reiki Kanji can therefore be read as meaning, *"Receiving Divine spiritually guided life force from the heavens into our body"*. The message being that human beings possess the ability to connect to these Divine energies and that through a *"medium"*, we can bring down and create *"heaven"* upon Earth. As is referenced on the Reiki Kanji by a second heaven existing under the *"clouds"*. This is *"spiritual wisdom"*.

REI

S
P
I
R
I
T
U
A
L

W
I
S
D
O
M

Heaven

Clouds

The veil between
Heaven & Earth

靈

Rain drops

Body/Container

Heaven

Medium

Earth

KI

L
I
F
E

F
O
R
C
E

氣

Steam produced by
the rays of the sun

A cooking pot

Grain of rice
expanding

SPIRITUALLY GUIDED LIFE FORCE ENERGY

An interpretation of the second part of the original meaning associated with the Reiki Kanji is as follows: *"KI..."*

- In Asian countries, *"rice"* is the main source or supply of energy. Another vital form of human sustenance, similar to the rain. The actual shape of this part of the symbol reflects an outward radiating energy.
- The *"steam produced by the rays of the sun"* represents the flow of our bodys Ki energy rising upwards towards the heavens.

When the imagery and meaning of the top Kanji, *'Rei'*, is combined with the bottom Kanji, *'Ki'*, we have *'Reiki'*. Its hidden symbolic message shows us that by:

66 *Using our body as a medium, we can connect to the Divine by activating our inner Ki and radiating this energy towards the heavens. This pours life force energy into our bodies.* 99

This is the nature of how we are all connected to the Source of all creation and how Reiki can be used to shine our true inner selves towards this creative-Source. The Source which some have come to know as God, or the god-consciousness, lies dormant within your own Heart and awaits your desire to be opened and explored.

REIKI TUMMO

Earlier in this book I mentioned the importance of learning a form of Kundalini Reiki and recommended that you be attuned to Reiki Tummo. You should now have a better understanding as to why activating your Kundalini is important. It is your bodys Ki energy that connects with the Divine Source of Reiki and once fully activated, this greatly improves your connection to Source and improves any and all other forms of Reiki channelling. The easiest and quickest way to fully activate your Ki energy is to receive the first two attunements in the Reiki Tummo system.

Reiki Tummo activates the dormant Kundalini energy that rests within your root Chakra and opens and cleanses all of your Chakras from root to crown. This means that instead of using only the Crown, Third Eye, Throat and Heart Chakras to channel Reiki, which is what is used for Usui Reiki and many other forms, you will be using the full power of your seven main Chakras simultaneously.

Reiki Tummo connects your body to the energies of Mother Earth and when we combine this energy flowing up through the Earth and our root with the Divine energy flowing down through our Crown, our channelling ability is significantly increased. So every time you channel Usui Reiki, you will automatically channel Reiki Tummo from the Earth through your Root, Sacral and Solar Plexus Chakras also.

If you are serious about mastering yourself and the many hundreds of Spiritual Chakras that exist above your head, you must first master your own body and energy field. Through activating your Kundalini you can achieve that self-mastery and fulfill your full potential. With Reiki Tummo you can achieve exactly that. Reiki Tummo is a very rare and almost unheard of spiritual practice that can help an individual take magnificent leaps forward in their personal growth and spiritual development. If you are serious about your spiritual path towards enlightenment, you should give serious consideration to learning Reiki Tummo.

Reiki Tummo is an advanced spiritual system that has been formulated by living enlightened Yogi, Master Irmansyah Effendi. The first two levels of Reiki Tummo can be learned at a distance over Skype and should you wish, you can continue on this same path towards achieving Yogi, or enlightenment. You can find a more detailed explanation of Reiki Tummo and full course details at *www.reikitummo.com/reiki-tummo/distant-learning.*

CHAPTER 32
UNDERSTANDING THE REIKI SYMBOLS

❝ *Whatever harm an enemy may do to an enemy, or a hater to a hater, an ill-directed mind inflicts on oneself a greater harm.* ❞
– Buddha

It is not essential to use the Reiki symbols in order to give a Reiki treatment, however the symbols students are attuned to in Reiki Second Degree, and the symbols passed on in higher level attunements, allow for greater versatility and increased power while channelling these higher vibrations of energy. As part of the Reiki tradition, the symbols you are given are sacred and should be treated with the up-most respect.

Many Reiki Teachers recommend that you should not keep copies of the symbols in a place where they may be discovered by anyone not attuned to that level of Reiki and that you should not share or speak their mantra with anyone uninitiated into Reiki. While this is a matter of personal preference, your relationship with the Reiki symbols is what is important and they should always be cherished within your heart.

Although some Reiki Practitioners and Masters have made the personal decision to share these Reiki symbols with the uninitiated public and many may be found online and in books, there are reasons why you may want to keep the Reiki symbols you were attuned to secret. For thousands of years, energy workers have understood the importance of keeping symbols secret. Some people believe the symbols may decrease in power if you share them with the uninitiated. While this in itself is not true, if you lose that sense of sacredness with your symbols or with Reiki in general, it could have a negative impact upon your channelling abilities. It's the relationship of sacredness you hold with the symbols that empowers your connection with them, not who's eyes may look upon them.

When we reach an even deeper level of Reiki, we come to realize that the symbols themselves are not important. The symbols have no power. They are only keys. The *real* power comes from your mind, heart and from the Source, not from the symbols. It is likely that the notion of keeping the Reiki symbols secret stems from the fact that Reiki was originally practised within a secret society, who's very nature involved keeping their practices secret. As with everything in Reiki, the choice is entirely yours. Just remember that there is a big difference between something being secret and something being sacred.

Each Reiki symbol is linked to a specific vibration of energy that can be used for different purposes. When you visualize a Reiki symbol, you change the frequency of energy you connect with. So some symbols are better suited for performing specific tasks than others, such as to heal physical, mental, emotional or spiritual imbalances. During the attunement process, the energies of each symbol descend and enter the student's mind and body and become linked to the appropriate symbols in the student's mind. From that moment onwards, whenever the student activates each symbol, the same energy that was linked to it during the attunement is activated and begins to flow. Each symbol is simply your personal key to channel that symbols specific frequency of healing energy.

When it comes to using each symbol, all that is necessary is to think of the symbol, or use one of the many other ways to activate it. This connects your body and mind to the specific frequency of energy associated with that symbol. At this point the Reiki energy begins to flow in through your Crown Chakra, down to the heart Chakra, through your arms and then flows through the Chakras in your palms.

When you use the Reiki symbols during a treatment, it is important to use the exact symbols you were given during your attunement, as these are the energetic keys that link your mind to the associated energies. There are different variations of the Reiki symbols that differ slightly in design, depending upon which

Reiki Master has completed your attunement. Mrs Takata herself, the Reiki Master that brought the Japanese tradition of Reiki to the Western world, didn't draw the symbols the same way each time she attuned a student. Out of the 22 Masters taught by Mrs Takata, slight differences between the symbols were given to each Master. This is why so many symbol variations currently exist. When a Reiki Master shows the Reiki symbols to a student and gives the attunement for that symbol, it is this specific version of the symbol that is imprinted upon the mind of the student. Which version of the symbol you are attuned to is not important, however using the symbol you were attuned to is important, as it is this symbol that creates your energetic connection to that specific frequency of healing energy.

ACTIVATING THE REIKI SYMBOLS

There are a number of ways to activate the energy associated with each Reiki symbol. You can draw the symbols on each of your hands or on your clients body, either with your middle finger or by visualization alone. You can also say their sacred mantra out loud or in your mind three times. Imagining a beam of light coming out your palm Chakra while drawing the symbols with your palm will work also. The intention to use a specific symbol is the main catalyst to activate that symbols healing energy and when you are more experienced, you can activate each symbol by simply intending to use them by will power alone.

You may also discover that these healing energies can activate themselves on their own accord, as our etheric bodies and subconscious can communicate with one another without our conscious awareness. While starting out, it will be easier to draw the symbols, with your middle finger or visually, in the exact process in which you were taught to. Each stroke at a time. You can also draw these on the body of the individual you are giving a treatment to. When you have become familiar with how to draw each symbol, you can easily and effectively visualize the entire symbol without having to draw it out one stroke at a time.

Once you have more experience and have developed a deeper relationship with the Reiki symbols, you can activate them by will alone, without the need of visualisations or mantras. Regardless of how you choose to connect with each symbol, remember that the symbols are merely keys that connect with each frequency of energy. Once you have established that connection, remove your mind, the desire to heal and your ego from your healing session and open and surrender your whole Heart to the Source of Reiki. Your whole heart consists of your Heart chakra, your physical Heart and your Inner Heart, which is where your spiritual essence resides. Surrendering simply involves stating your intention to do so while speaking and feeling this intention direct from your heart. Then simply direct a continuous sweet smile to your whole Heart. This helps to release the body chemicals necessary for a more relaxed state and deeper and stronger connection to the Source of Reiki.

THREE TIPS TO HELP WHILE CHANNELLING REIKI

- Your body should be loose and relaxed to help maximize the flow of Reiki energy through your body into your client. Tense muscles will reduce the natural flow of energy through your body.
- Keep your mind clear and free of all thoughts. The only time you should be mentally focused is when you are preparing yourself to give a treatment, or drawing or visualizing the symbols you are using during that treatment. Once your intention and the connection to the energy has been established, clear your mind, feel the connection with the energy, and let it flow freely, feeling this connection through your whole Heart.
- Love and compassion are the two prime feelings one should project towards the energy they are connecting with. If you are feeling any negative emotions, it would be unwise to conduct a Reiki treatment, as you may project these negative energies from your own energy field into your clients energy field and body.

CHAPTER 33
USUI REIKI I SYMBOL
THE POWER SYMBOL - CHOKU REI

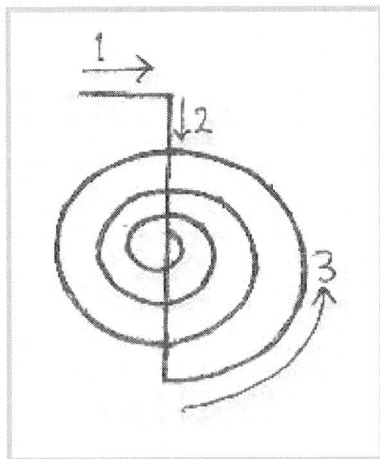

Meaning and command: 'Put all the power of the universe here now! By Imperial Decree'.
Japanese Name: Cho Ku Rei
Pronunciation: Cho Koo Ray
Intention: Power Switch
Uses: Manifestation, energy empowerment, physical healing, aura or room cleansing, protection, physical energy boost, alleviates physical pain...

Explanation: The Power Symbol is usually discovered during your first attunement, depending on your teacher, and this can be used for everything and anything. The Power Symbol can be used:

- **To cleanse impurities from food or drink**. Take a moment to place your hands over your food and drink and ask that all toxins and impurities be removed.
- **Around your body to shield against negative energies**. Imagine you are standing in an invisible cube

171

and visualize the power symbol on each of the six sides. One at your feet, your head, and on each of the four sides of your energy field. Ask that you be cleansed and protected from all negative energies.

- *'If you complete the higher degree attunements, placing it over any of the other symbols will increase that symbols power.'*
- **To seal healing energies into the body after a treatment**. Using Choku Rei near the end of your treatments, on each of your seven main Chakras, asking that the healing energy of Reiki be sealed within each Chakra with love and light.
- **To clear a room of negativity and make it a sacred place**. Similar to cleansing and protecting your bodys' energy field, put a Choku Rei on each of the walls in a room, the floor and ceiling and ask that the room be cleansed of all negative energies and filled with loving white light.
- **To protect your car, home, children or body from negativity and harm**. Place the power symbol upon the brow of your child, surrounding their energy field, or surrounding your car, asking that they remain safe and protected from unwanted negative energies.
- **To empower and cleanse crystals and stones used for healing**. Placing your stones/crystals in direct sunlight or moonlight will cleanse your stones/crystals of negative energies, making them neutral. Although you can also use Choku Rei for this. Then you may charge your stones/crystals with positive energy using any of the Reiki symbols you have been attuned to.
- **To protect yourself from verbal and emotional confrontations or psychic attack**. Imagine the power symbol between you and another individual during an argument or uncomfortable exchange, asking that you remain unaffected by the negative energies being directed towards you.
- **When shaking hands or hugging** another person to

block the transference of their negative energies into your own energy field and body. Again, visualize this symbol on your hand or between your two bodies.

- **For manifesting goals.** Write your goals on a piece of paper and empower them using Choku Rei.
- **To boost your confidence and self-esteem.** All you have to do is use it while setting your intention.

The Power Symbol can literally be used for anything else you can think of. The only limit to using the Power Symbol is the limit you place upon your own imagination.

This symbol will intensify the flow of Reiki during a treatment and is also used to seal the Reiki energy into the client at the end of a treatment or attunement. The Power Symbol can be used to empower any of the other symbols or can be used by itself during a treatment. The top horizontal line represents the energy of the Divine Source. The line coming down represents the energy coming down to earth and down the spinal column. The spiral represents the earth energy. The spiral then crosses the vertical line seven times representing the seven main chakras of the human body and spirals around the aura or energy field of the person channelling.

The *'power'* of the power symbol is not to be confused with the power to influence or control the behaviour of other people. It is the power to increase the natural flow of the Reiki energy and to empower all other Reiki symbols. It can be used multiple times during a Reiki treatment and placed upon any Chakra, or any other part of the human body. Each time you use this symbol, the Reiki energy will increase in power, strength and flow. If you are sensitive to energy, you will be able to feel an instant, yet gentle, increase to the flow of energy through your body and out your palms. As physical disharmony in the body is often rooted to an emotional, mental or spiritual imbalance, it is unlikely that the power symbol will be used by itself once you have completed the higher level Reiki attunements.

CHAPTER 34

USUI REIKI II SYMBOLS
THE MENTAL/EMOTIONAL SYMBOL – SEI HEKI

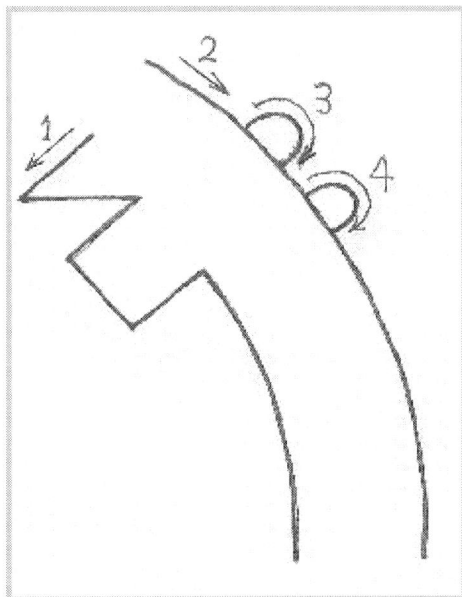

Meaning and command: 'The key to the universe' *(or)* 'man and god becoming one' *(or)* 'I am the keeper of your soul.'
Japanese Name: Sei He Ki
Pronunciation: Say Hay Key
Intention: Emotional balance and mental equilibrium
Uses: Psychic protection, to balance both sides of the brain, helps with addictions, helps creating a new habit, heals relationship issues, heals negative energies attached to past traumatic events when used with the distance symbol, removes negative energies, creates balance and harmony…

Explanation: This symbol represents balance and harmony and helps to heal emotional issues. The Emotional/Mental symbol can be used for:

- Dealing with feelings of fear, anger, anxiety, depression, nervousness, and stress etc.
- Helping any type of addiction, such as smoking, alcoholism, drug abuse, weight issues etc..
- Helping to calm the emotions and nerves.
- Releasing current emotional issues attached to traumatic events in your past.
- Psychological healing.
- Memory loss: e.g. where are my house keys, why did I enter this room, what was I just going to say.
- Finding lost objects.
- Healing relationship issues.
- Bringing harmony and peace.
- Improving mental concentration during exams, tests or while studying.
- Affirmations: repeating the name of this symbol with any positive affirmation helps that affirmation penetrate the subconscious mind with greater ease.

When using the mental/emotional symbol, as with any other symbol for that matter, remember that it's energy is directed in accordance with your thoughts and intentions. Remember to include, *"for the highest and greatest good"* at the end of the intention you set before you start channelling.

A powerful way to use this symbol is to draw/visualize it on the heart Chakra, your emotional center, while giving a treatment, and using it on the head with the various hand positions you were taught. The Sei He Ki symbol works by removing blockages in the aura and helps heal an individual psychologically by working on their higher levels of consciousness. Many physical illnesses are the direct result of emotional and mental imbalances which one may not be aware of and science has begun to realize this. The Sei He Ki Symbol helps to tackle these physical illnesses at their mental/emotional root. For this reason, it can be advantageous to always use the Sei Hei Ki Symbol when giving a treatment.

It's not uncommon for the client, or even the Reiki Practitioner, to become suddenly emotional when using this symbol. This is a sign of the blockage being worked on and rising to the surface to be dealt with by the individual. Using this symbol helps to bridge the gap between the physical body and the emotional/mental bodies, which helps to harmonize the subconscious with the physical body to promoting balance, peace and harmony in ones state of mind, body and being.

As mentioned in the *'uses'* section, this symbol can also be used to heal past events and experiences that may still be causing an individual emotional or mental anguish in the present time. To do so, one should first use the distance symbol, empower it with the Power Symbol, and then draw/visualize Sei Hei Ki over it. Then Choku Rei over that to add extra power. All with the intention of sending healing energies to a specific past event to clear the negative mental/emotional energy that has persisted since one experienced that event.

When you are performing a channelling session, remember to always use the highest frequency Reiki symbol first. If you were a Reiki Master for instance and have been attuned to the Dai Ko Myo symbol, always visualize this symbol first before using any other. This helps you connect with the highest vibration of healing energy before you channel into your client or towards your desired target.

THE DISTANCE SYMBOL - HON SHA ZE SHO NEN

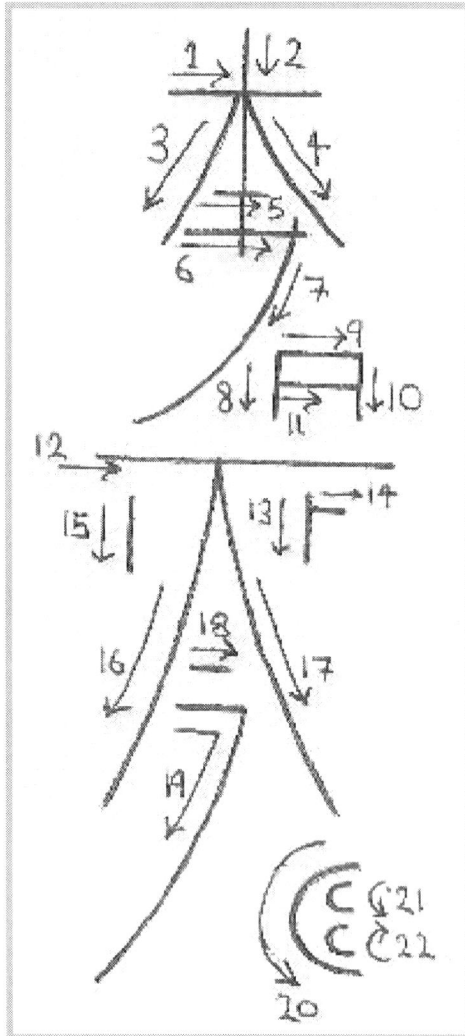

Meaning and command: 'The Buddha in me reaches out to the Buddha in you to promote peace and enlightenment' *(or)* 'No past, no present, no future'.
Japanese Name: Hon Sha Ze Sho Nen

Pronunciation: Hon Sha Zay Show Nen
Intention: Timelessness connection
Uses: Directing healing to a past event or a future event, sending healing to an absent client, releasing past trauma, healing karma, performing exorcisms on a person or object, releasing a trapped spirit from the material world and helping them pass over into the light.

Explanation: The Hon Sha Ze Sho Nen Symbol is used to send healing energies to people, events, situations, and places that are not in your physical vicinity. This symbol can be used:

- When sending absent healing to a client not in your presence.
- To send healing to someone that may be in a different room, city, country, or dimension/world.
- To send energy to a past event that may still be causing mental/emotional issues, *(would be used with the Mental/Emotional Symbol.)*
- To send energy to a future situation or event, such as a job interview, dental visit, exam, meeting, or any other future event that you, or someone else, will attend.
- To send healing energy to any conflict situation, such as a war. Remember to send healing energies to the both sides, not just one, as all good relationships involve the balance of both parties.
- To send helpful energy to a disaster situation anywhere in the world, such as a flood, a tsunami, an earthquake, a fire, a famine, drought, or any other suffering etc.
- To send Reiki to any individual, anywhere, as long as they have given their permission.
- To send energy to pets or wild animals when touching such creatures would be unsafe and inappropriate. Remember to ask the animal in your mind that they may receive the healing energy only if they wish to.
- To help your vegetables or plants in your garden to grow. Remember to be specific about where the energy goes as you can also send it to the weeds.

- To release spirits from an object, house or area.
- To complete an exorcism and to remove an entity or spirit that may be inhabiting a person. Remember to cleanse and protect yourself with an energy circle and ask your Reiki or spirit guides to take the entity to the light, with love, light and blessings.

The Hon Sha Ze Sho Nen Symbol is especially powerful when used with the Se He Ki symbol and empowered with Choku Rei while your client visualizes a past traumatic event. This helps to send Reiki energy to these past events to heal any emotional issues that have persisted since the experience. The healing energy of Reiki knows no bounds and is not restricted by time, space, or distance. Sending Reiki by distance healing is just as strong and effective as if the client were receiving a hands-on treatment. You can also use this symbol with all the other symbols to program the Reiki energy, so that it may be received continuously or at a certain time. For example, instead of completing a daily healing on yourself for an hour, you can spend one hour on Sunday programming Reiki to send you healing energies at 9PM for the next 7 days. This symbol can also be used during past life regressions to help heal and release Karmic issues that have been brought over from your previous lifetimes into your current life cycle.

When sending distance healing, the only necessary tool you need is your mind. The Reiki energy is activated and sent through thought and intention, so it is not necessary to do anything with your hands. Your hands can be on your knees, can be clasped or can be held in prayer position. If you prefer having an object to focus upon when sending distance healing, you can use any of the means described in the next paragraph.

HOW TO USE THE DISTANCE HEALING SYMBOL

Sending distance healing is a simple process and involves almost exactly the same procedure as giving a normal hands-on treatment. When sending healing energies using this symbol, always establish the connection between the distance symbol and the person, event or situation you wish to send distance healing to once you have performed Gassho and Reiji-Ho. If you are sending distance healing to a person you may, if you wish, hold a picture of that person in your hands, write their name on a piece of paper and hold this in your hands, or use a teddy bear or pillow to act as point of focus for your mind.

Once you have established your connection for sending this person distance healing, set your intention to send Reiki to that person. Your intention should always be to send Reiki, "*For their highest and greatest good only.*" This intention ensures your client only receives what is best for them and ensures you do not accumulate negative karma as a result of creating unforeseen circumstances for your client.

Once you have set your intention and visualized the Distance Symbol, you can then visualize the Choku Reiki Symbol on top of the Distance Healing Symbol. This will empower the Distance Symbol. You can then visualize the Mental/Emotional Symbol over the top of these two symbols, then finally visualize/draw another Choku Reiki Symbol over that to empower the Mental/Emotional Symbol.

This is especially powerful if you wish to focus on sending Mental/Emotional healing to your client at a distance. Of course, you can simply visualize/draw the Distance Symbol and then empower that with a Choku Rei Symbol and use just these two symbols. It depends what you are sending Reiki for and what your intentions are as each symbol has its own specific purpose.

Once you have done so, simply relax your body as much as possible and keep your mind clear of thoughts during the session. If thoughts do enter your mind, allow them to pass out your head without analysing them. Here are a few of the many ways you can send Distance Healing to a client or event:

- Holding a picture of your target between your hands.

- Writing your targets name on a piece of paper and holding this in your hands.
- Using a mannequin and holding this in your hands or sitting it in front of you. Say the persons name three times, visualize/draw the Distance Symbol over the teddy bear or pillow, set your intention, use any other symbols you wish to, and then visualize sending it Reiki. Then do a standard treatment using all the hand positions on the mannequin, intending that Reiki be sent to each Chakra position on that person. Once you have established your connection with the teddy bear or pillow, it is also possible to do Byosen Scanning on that representation and feel where energy needs to be sent to that individual. Intending to feel your clients energy through the mannequin is the intention to set yourself before Byosen Scanning it.
- If you wish to send Reiki to a large object or place, such as the planet or a country, visualize this in your mind and gradually make it smaller until it fits in your hands, then hold this imaginary image in your hands and let the Reiki flow to it. Of course, you can also write the planet or place on a piece of paper and hold this between your hands. Your intention is what is important.
- You can also imagine the person in front of you and hold your hands up in the direction in which you imagine the person to be. Draw the Distance Symbol over them and any other symbols you wish to use, then set your intention and let the Reiki flow.
- You can send Reiki with your eyes open or shut, so you can also send a distance treatment while sitting in public or while driving a car. Any object can be used as a point of focus to establish a connection to the person you wish to send Distance Healing to. Establish your connection with the Distance Symbol, the object and the person, say the name of the person you wish to channel to, then keep both hands on the object as you channel Reiki. Add any of the other Reiki symbols if you wish.

- You can also use the Distance healing symbol to send Reiki to individuals you have known in the past, to people on TV, to political figures, to famous people, or to anyone that is injured or otherwise in need of help. If sending Reiki to a person who you are not in contact with and who can therefore not accept or refuse to receive Reiki, always include at the end of your intention a statement asking their permission. For example, you might say, *"Please send Reiki to this individual if it be for their highest and greatest good only, if they agree to accept these healing energies."* If it is not in this persons highest and greatest good to receive these healing energies, their etheric bodies and higher consciousness's will not allow it and they will not be affected by the Reiki energy you send them.

Everyone can have a different experience with Reiki and it can be advantageous to experiment with these healing energies and symbols. One particular experiment that has reportedly had good results is sending Distance Healing, for the highest and greatest good, to Jesus, Buddha, God, the full moon, planet Earth, Pagan Gods, your spirit guides, your Reiki guides, angels, and so on. Those who have done such a thing have reported that they have received tremendous healing back from these spiritual beings. Additionally, it also helps create a stronger connection between you and these beings, so that your prayers or magical workings are empowered further in the future. However you should keep in mind that the Divine Source, the Creative Source of all existence, is the most powerful of all.

Remember that Reiki can do no harm to an individual, as this is the very life force energy from the creative source itself. Remember to *always* be respectful of ones free will, as free will is a vital part of ones personal growth and spiritual development. In situations where this is not possible, always include the statement, *"Please send Reiki to this individual if it be for their highest and greatest good only, if they agree to accept these healing energies."* Generally however, it is customary practice to ask the individual if they are willing to receive Reiki before sending it to them.

SENDING DISTANCE HEALING AS A GROUP

Hands-on Reiki sessions can be given by any number of Reiki practitioners and there are a number of advantages to having more than one Reiki Practitioner working on a client. Having six Practitioners giving a hands-on treatment to the same individual all at the same time for 10 minutes, would be the equivalent to receiving a one-hour treatment from one Reiki Practitioner. Distance healings are no different and with sufficient numbers, there is nothing to stop 100 Reiki Practitioners all sending Distance Healing to the same person, event, or situation simultaneously. Powerful results can be achieved by a group of Reiki II Practitioners giving Distance Healings at the same time and doing so is as simple as each individual following the previous mentioned steps for sending Reiki Healings at a distance. Once attuned to higher levels, your abilities increase.

Sitting in a circle, although this itself is not necessary, place a picture of the person in the middle of the group, or a piece of paper with your goal or recipients name written upon it in the middle. Then have everyone follow the procedure of connecting to this picture or name using the Distance Symbol. Remember to say the command, Hon Sha Ze Sho Nen, three times as you draw or visualize it placed upon the picture or name. Add the Choku Rei power symbol on top of that, then the Mental/Emotional Symbol, and then a final Choku Rei symbol on top of the Mental/Emotional Symbol. Making four symbol in total. Remember to say the names of each symbol three times as you draw/visualize them. Then say the persons name three times stating, *"I send Reiki to {insert intention}, for their highest and greatest good only."*

Sending group Reiki does not even need to be done by Practitioners while in the same room. Any number of Reiki

Practitioners can send Distance Healings together at the same time when each person is in a different room, city or country. Simply agree a time when you will all send a Distance Healing and each follow the previously mentioned steps. Remember, Reiki works through intention, so you can use your imagination to come up with other ways of achieving the same result. The real key to success is your mind, your heart and your belief that what you are doing will be successful.

CHAPTER 35
USUI MASTER SYMBOL
THE MASTER SYMBOL - DAI KO MYO

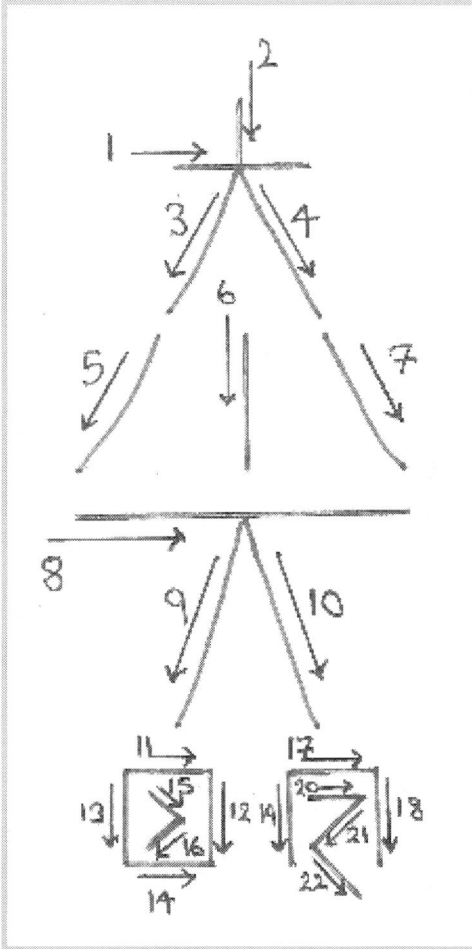

Meaning and command: 'Great being of the Universe, shine on me be my friend' *(or)* 'Eastern House of the great beaming light'.
Japanese Name: Dai Ko Myo
Pronunciation: Die Koe Me-Oh
Intention: Enlightenment

Uses: Empowers, purifies and strengthens, soul/spirit healing, oneness, enhances all previous symbols, used to bless everything...

Explanation: The Master Symbol should be used with every healing, if you have been initiated to this level, and should be the first symbol used before using any of the previous symbols. Include *'Hon Sha Ze Sho Nen'* after, if using the distance symbol to send absent healing. The Master Symbol represents the combined energies of all the previous symbols. In *'The Encyclopaedia of Eastern Philosophy and Religion'*, it states this symbol is a Zen expression for ones own true nature, or Buddha nature. Of which one becomes knowledgeable and aware in the experience of enlightenment. As the Dai Ko Myo symbol represents empowerment, intuition and spiritual connection, it is especially useful to meditate upon when you are alone, as this can lead to you receiving psychic impulses/messages and help you reach a new level of consciousness and understanding as to your direction and purpose in life.

Using this symbol in treatments sends Reiki towards the root of all sickness, illness and dis-ease by sending it to the higher spiritual self. Dai Ko Myo is one of the highest vibrations of energy in Usui Reiki and is said to contain the energies of all the other Usui Reiki symbols. Our limited human understanding can not fully grasp this power, however we know the magic of this symbols energy to be effective and deeply transformative.

The Master Symbol helps to create a stronger connection between our physical self and our higher self, allowing the increased wisdom and power of the creative-source to manifest directly upon the physical plain. Using Dai Ko Myo in your treatments will greatly intensify and focus the Reiki energy to your target, leading to positive results for your client or target. When using Dai Ko Myo, the healer is safe and protected from unwanted lower negative energies and remains firmly grounded.

All of the other Reiki symbols you have discovered are enhanced by Dai Ko Myo, which increases the quality and effectiveness of each one. This helps to bring a greater and deeper level of wholeness, clarity and fulfillment to your life when channelling this symbols energy regularly. To intensify Dai Ko Myo further, the Choku Rei Power Symbol can be visualized/drawn over the Master Symbol to empower it further. Once attuned to the Master symbol, always use it first before the other symbols and visualize it before and after using the Distance Symbol to maximize the intensity of the energy associated with the Distance Symbol. This symbol is used:

- On a spiritual level to heal the soul.
- Before all other symbols to empower them.
- To bring in a higher vibration of healing frequency.
- To develop ones intuition, spiritual awareness, and personal growth and development.
- During all healing treatments and during meditation.
- To increase the power and effectiveness of the Reiki I and Reiki II symbols
- To effectively clear stones, crystals, or objects of negative energy.
- To develop ones consciousness and feeling of oneness with all.
- To improve spiritual guidance for developing ones true self and exploring the essence of being.
- For blessing anything with a far more powerful frequency of energy.
- For empowering ones goals, or oneself, with these higher frequency energies.
- For opening ones Heart and increasing feelings of unconditional love and compassion.

When channelling Reiki, always visualize/draw the symbol with the highest frequency of vibration first, before visualizing/drawing any of the other symbols. This ensures your connection to the Source of Reiki is as strong as possible.

CHAPTER 36
MANIFESTATION - EMPOWERING YOUR GOALS

❝ Let us rise up and be thankful, for if we didn't learn a lot today, at least we learned a little, and if we didn't learn a little, at least we didn't get sick, and if we got sick, at least we didn't die; so, let us be thankful. ❞ **– Buddha**

Once attuned to second degree Usui Reiki and above, you are able to channel energy into the past and forward into the future. By reinforcing a thought or intention with the positive energy of Reiki, you can attract what you truly desire into your life. If you have a specific goal you wish to achieve, or wish to manifest something into your life, there is a simple and effective process for helping your desires come to fruition. Whatever your goal may be, whether to receive a promotion, find a job, improve a relationship, expand your social circles, connect to a spirit guide, to open your third eye and so on, take a piece of paper or card and write your name upon it. Then on the same piece of paper, write down a name for your goal, or write a description of the goal you wish to achieve or have manifest in your life. If your goal involves a specific time and date in the future, write that down also. It's important to be specific about what you desire.

Now draw all the symbols you have learned onto the same piece of paper or card, starting with the Master symbols, then the Distance Symbol, the Sei Heki mental/emotional Symbol and then followed by the Choku Rei Power Symbol. Remember to empower every symbol further with the Choku Rei Symbol. Once you have done this, keep it in a safe place and continue to Reiki it for 15 to 20 minutes or so each day.

Carry this piece of paper with you everywhere you go so that it's in constant contact with your body's energy field and give it Reiki whenever you have a spare moment. Continue to actively work towards achieving your goal in your daily life and if that goal is in harmony with your highest and greatest good, which should form part of your intention, you will achieve it. Remember, your thoughts are reinforced by your emotions and your energy, so focus your thoughts, emotions and energy on only positives. Your mind will create what you intend it to create.

In truth, there is no one set way to manifest your goals using Reiki. The only necessities are a focused thought reinforced by the energy of Reiki. Visualizations and rituals may be conducted, however they are not the source of Reiki's power. They only provide the student with a means of focus so Reiki energy may be directed towards manifesting that desire in the future. The goal is to be able to will our future to happen using our thoughts and energy while relying on intuitive guidance.

While on your spiritual path, it is also important to consider the spiritual implications of manifesting your future. While certain choices and actions may seem kind and logical in our head, the human brain limits our connection to the Source. That connection can only be fully experienced through opening and surrendering our whole Heart to the Divine Source. In doing so, we become increasingly aware of the guidance being sent towards us. And it's that intuitive/Divine guidance that leads us each towards our unique life purpose.

While we have physical human desires for what we want to attract into our lives, this is not always what is best for us in a spiritual sense. A good way for energy workers to be aware of the spiritual consequences of their actions is to make use of some form of divination. The most popular and easy to learn method is the Tarot cards, which are relatively simple to learn and highly effective. With them, we can have a clearer picture of how our energy work is going to affect our future and what the spiritual and energetic consequences of our choices will be.

The Karma returned to you is based upon your results, not your intentions. Therefore ensuring your good intentions yield good results is of prime importance for any energy worker.

CHAPTER 37
USUI MASTER-TEACHER SYMBOLS
TIBETAN MASTER SYMBOL – DAI KO MIO

❝ *The foot feels the foot when it's touched by the ground, like the heart feels the heart when it's no longer bound.* ❞
– Ricky Mathieson

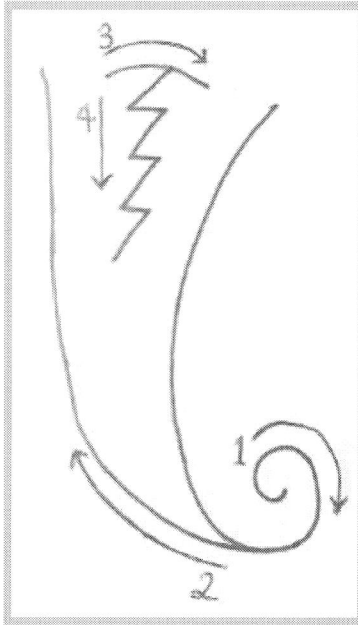

Meaning and command: 'Take us back to God' *(or)* 'The lotus sailing to enlightenment'
Name: Dai Ko Mio
Pronunciation: Die Koe Mee Oh
Intention: Spiritual Enlightenment
Uses: Holds similar characteristics as the Usui Dai Ko Myo and is used mainly during attunements. However it can also be used on its own for healing and expanding ones consciousness. The Tibetan Dai Ko Mio has one of the highest and finest vibrations and can penetrate deeply at an etheric and spiritual level.

Explanation: This symbols high and fine vibratory frequency helps to deeply heal our energy bodies and our higher spiritual selves. It also helps to bring the mind and body into balance and harmony. It is most commonly used during Healing Attunements and Teacher student Attunements as part of the violet breath, however it is also a powerful tool for cleansing and opening our energy channels and is effective at cleansing and energizing the chakras. This makes the Dai Ko Mio symbol fantastic for healing your clients as well as working on developing yourself.

The Tibetan Dai Ko Mio can assist in healing a wide range of holistic issues and does so quickly and at a far deeper level. Because of the penetrating deepness associated with this symbol, it can also be used effectively with Psychic Surgery or to cleanse crystals of negative energies. You may be aware of a pulling sensation in your hands or body when using this symbol, as it literally pulls negative energy from the body very effectively.

Using this symbol with the technique is effective at any moment, not just attunements, and you can use it in this way to send healing energies into an individuals energy field, physical body, spiritual self, or specific organ or area of dis-ease. All matters of dis-ease, whether physical, mental, emotional or spiritual in nature, can be effectively cleansed using the Tibetan Dai Ko Mio. When used during a healing attunement, which can be incorporated into a standard Reiki treatment, it's effects are especially powerful and it's this power that allows a Reiki healer to target negative energy blockages at their root.

This symbol can be used to deeply penetrate any aspect of a persons being and can be used to activate and open the Kundalini and to cleanse the main energy channel that runs up the spine and out the Crown. **WARNING**: If you have not received the proper training and attunement, **DO NOT** try to activate your Kundalini yourself. If your main energy channel is not opened first, you could cause your Kundalini to activate prematurely and in my experience, that will create all sorts of problems for you that can have severe negative consequences.

TIBETAN FIRE SERPENT

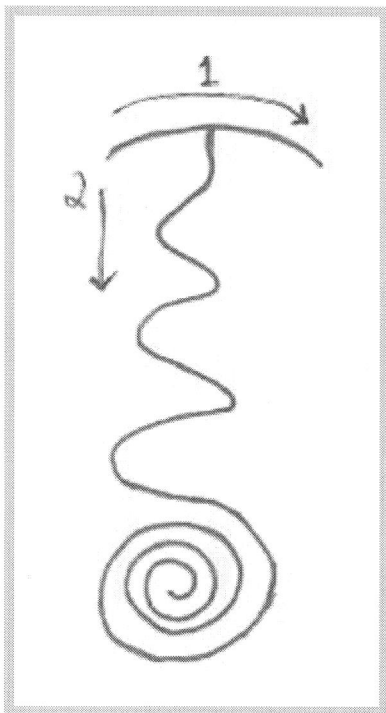

Name: Tibetan Fire Serpent, or Fire Dragon
Intention: Opening Kundalini & linking the seven main Chakras
Uses: Used during student attunements, healing attunements, or standard Reiki treatments.

Explanation: The Fire Serpent symbol represents the sleeping serpent, coiled at the root chakra at the base of the spine. It is drawn down the spine at the beginning of an attunement, or healing attunement, and opens the Chakras of the body to prepare ones energy system to receive the attunement energies. This allows the Reiki energy to better flow into the student receiving the attunement as all the Chakras are opened and linked together. When used during an attunement, the curved line *(stroke.1)* is drawn over the crown chakra. It's then motioned down the spine using the palm of the hand and spirals in a clockwise direction at the base of the spine. This helps to ground the attunement energies from the root chakra, down the legs and into the lower body. Typically, it should be drawn down the back of the persons spine who is receiving it, however it can also be used on the front of the body with the intention of it flowing down the spine.

The Fire Serpent symbol is believed to unify the body and mind and works on activating the bodies Kundalini energy that's coiled itself in the Root Chakra. As it opens our Chakras and energy channels, it is especially useful at pulling negative energy from our body, similar to the Tibetan Dai Ko Mio. It is important to note however, that the Fire Serpent does not fully open the main energy pathway running up the spine, neither does it fully activate the dormant Kundalini energy safely. To achieve that, I would recommend being attuned to Reiki Tummo. The sole purpose of those first two Tummo attunements is to open the main energy channel of the spine and then fully activate the sleeping Kundalini energy in the root chakra.

You can also draw/visualize the Fire Serpent, as you would any other symbol, when giving a standard Reiki treatment by simply drawing it on your palms, your clients Chakra, or in the air above your client. Using both the Tibetan Symbols in your healing sessions will penetrate the body deeply and heal your client on a far deeper energetic level than the Reiki symbols taught in the first few levels of Usui Reiki.

CHAPTER 38
THE ANTAHKARANA - TIBETAN HEALING SYMBOLS

Every experience, no matter how bad it seems, holds within it a blessing of some kind. The goal is to find it. **– Buddha**

The four Antahkarana symbols included in this manual are ancient healing symbols that were traditionally used in Tibetan healing temples and they can be used in conjunction with Reiki. These four symbols can strengthen Reiki energy and help to provide access to higher vibrations of energy and they are said to enhance meditation as well as all other forms of intention or spiritual practice. Usually purple in colour and printed on cotton, although any colour will do, they can be placed over your client on areas needing more healing, or where there are extra stubborn energy blockages you wish to have removed. They will work by themselves or you can place your hands over them and channel Reiki into your symbol of choice also.

The Antahkarana have been reported to speed up the healing process and improve ones rate of recovery and a copy of the symbols, or the ones printed in this manual, can be placed underneath your Reiki treatment couch, on the wall of your treatment area, or sat on during meditation or self-treatments. There are no attunements for the Antahkarana, so anyone can make use of them. Although knowledge of the Antahkarana in the Western world is limited, the Antahkarana is the spiritual cord that links your Crown chakra *(7th chakra)* to your Divine chakra *(8th chakra)* and it's working on improving this connection that gives access to the higher healing energies of the Divine 8th chakra and beyond.

The two large single Antahkarana symbols represent Yin & Yang, the female and the male energies. The larger of the two is the Yin, the female energy that shines its healing energy in a passive and gentle way. The smaller of the two is the yang, the male energy. Being the masculine energy, it's nature is therefore more direct, focused and penetrating. Either one can be used for treatments, meditations or on a Reiki Crystal Grid and you should use your intuition to decide which to use, depending upon the specific purpose of your healing session.

The Sacred Cross, or the Cosmic Cross as it's also known, is made of seven symbols crossing each other, representing the seven main chakras. This symbol will purify your own energy and can be used to open the heart more to the Divine Source of Reiki. The square multiple symbols, totalling 16 in number, help to break-up blocked energy and help your bodies Ki energy flow smoothly throughout your body with minimal resistance. You should keep in mind that the Sacred Cross can also scatter your energy, so it is always recommended that you follow its use with the single male symbol to keep the energy more focused and balanced. This will help to keep your physical and energy bodies balanced and more grounded to Mother Earth.

Experimenting meditating on each of the Antahkarana at a time can also offer healing and guidance and it is especially useful to meditate with an Antahkarana placed upon the crown of your head, near where your spiritual cord can be found. Meditating on each one at a time with your eyes opened, relaxed and gazing upon each image, with your body still and mind clear, can result in guidance and insight of a spiritual nature as it helps open our consciousness further. Alternatively, try meditating on a symbol for 30 minutes with it placed upon your head and be aware of the feeling in the air just above your crown chakra. This can help you reach a deeper level through your meditation work and can help to establish a connection with your Divine 8th chakra with time. Be aware however, that this could take some time with lots of regular practice.

- You will find the various Antahkarana on the pages that follow and can purchase professionally printed cotton tapestries of each symbol from the internet.

YIN – THE FEMALE ENERGY

The feminine Antahkarana has a more gentle energy than it's male counterpart and helps create greater receptivity to guidance and energy. The energy associated with this symbol helps one harness powerful energies that are less direct and you can feel the Yin energy within your body as a cold energy when you are channelling Reiki.

YANG – THE MALE ENERGY

The masculine opposite of the Yin is the Yang, which helps create a deeply penetrating and strong focus of healing energy that is more direct than the passive energies of the Yin. The Chakras are brought into balance through using this symbol and you can feel the Yang energy within your body as a hot energy when channelling Reiki.

THE SACRED CROSS OR COSMIC CROSS

The Sacred Cross, or the Cosmic Cross as it is also known, helps create a space of purity and maintains the sacredness of your working area. This can be a good symbol to place upon the wall of your therapy room to neutralize any negative energies. This symbol can also help to improve your relationship with your higher Reiki guides when channelling Reiki.

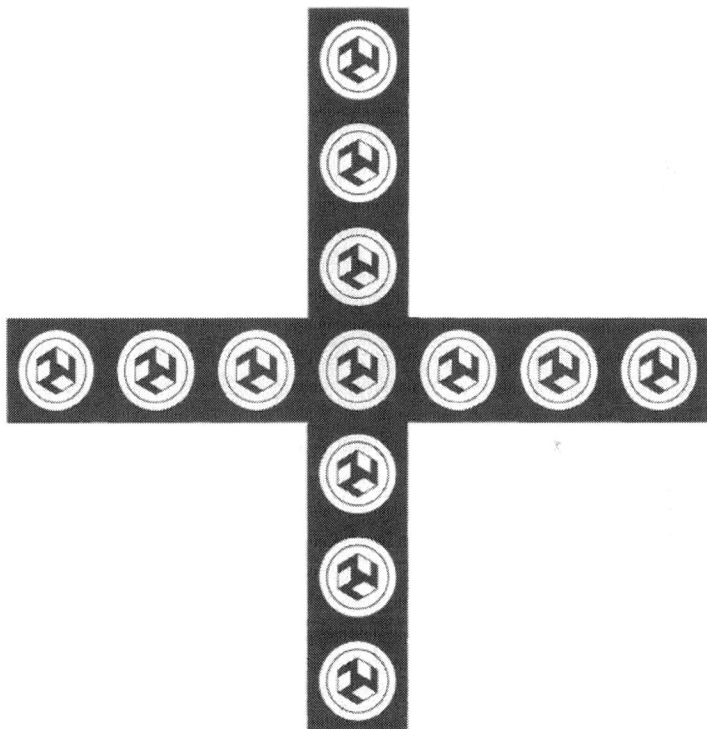

MULTIPLE ANTAHKARANA

The Multiple Antahkarana is used to break up energy blockages within the body and is an effective tool for releasing any kind of negative energy block within your physical body or one of your many energy bodies. It is also good for helping those with difficult emotional and mental issues that one may be experiencing and can be used with the other Antahkarana.

PART 4:

ATTUNEMENTS

"The way is not in the sky. The way is in the heart." – **Buddha**

CHAPTER 39
ATTUNEMENTS & CLEANSING PERIOD

❝ Before giving, the mind of the giver is happy; while giving, the mind of the giver is made peaceful; and having given, the mind of the giver is uplifted. ❞ – Buddha

Reiki can be learned by everyone and anyone regardless of age, gender or religion, and offers a safe and effective holistic approach to healthcare. You need no experience, no prior knowledge and need make no preparations before learning how to channel Reiki. You only need the desire to discover something new and the willingness to open yourself to the Divine Source of Reiki and the very force of creation itself. Reiki is not something we learn with intellect alone. It's a knowledge and deep knowing in our heart that comes only through personal experience.

Before being able to channel the energies of Reiki, one must receive an attunement from a fully qualified Reiki Teacher. This is to properly open your bodies own energy channels to improve their connection to Reiki. This helps to increase the natural flow of Reiki from the Source and through your body.

The Reiki attunements you receive at every level are powerful and will increasingly open your Crown Chakra further to improve your minds connection with the Divine healing energies of Reiki. What this does is open your mind, body and energy pathways wider, so that more life force energy can flow through your body. The attunement process can be different for every individual, as we are each currently at a different point in our personal spiritual journey and in our physical development.

During your attunement, some may have mystical experiences, see colours, have visions, experience body sensations such as tingling in the head or body, feel a sensation of peace, temporary emotional releases, floating sensations and some may experience nothing at all. It is important to know that if you do not feel anything during your attunement, your attunement has still been successful as the attunement process never fails to work, provided it is given by a fully qualified Reiki Master Teacher. Everyone's experience is as unique as the spiritual path they are on. Once you have been attuned at each level of Reiki, that attunement is with you for life and your connection to those energies is activated by intention and will.

One thing you may experience after your attunement is an increase in your psychic ability and an improved connection with nature. This is quite normal and is something you would be encouraged to develop if you decide to be attuned to the higher degrees of Reiki. The Reiki energy is intelligent in nature and each individual will only receive what they are capable of receiving at that time. So the attunement process will always give each individual exactly what is necessary for that person and no more. It is this intelligence of the Reiki energy that contributes towards everyone having a different experience.

When you receive any Reiki attunement, the vibration of your body raises to the vibrational level associated with the energy connected to you during your attunement. As everyone's body vibrates at a lower level of frequency before receiving a Reiki attunement, your body will naturally have to adjust to this higher vibration. As a result, it is perfectly normal to experience '*temporary*' and '*mild*' physical or emotional reactions as your body adjusts to this new higher level of vibration. This is known as your *21-Day-Cleansing-Period*.

The *21-Day-Cleansing-Period,* also referred to as the *healing-crisis*, is a process everyone who receives attunement goes through and it plays a normal and natural part in healing your mind, body and Spirit. During these 21-days, the Reiki energy works its way through each of your seven main Chakras. One Chakra each day at a time. After one week, the process is said to continue a further two times, cleansing and healing each Chakra in the process. As everyone is different, and we are all at a different level of balance before receiving an attunement, the 21-Day cleansing period can last less than 21-Days or longer.

WHAT YOU MAY EXPERIENCE DURING THE 21-DAYS

As everyone is at a different point in their spiritual journey and may be harboring varying levels of negative energy blocking their energy pathways, everyone's experiences will be different and will last a varying length of time. Some of the experiences you may undergo after your attunement could be any of the following:

- Flu like symptoms including headaches, a runny or blocked nose, mild aches and pains.
- Insomnia and restlessness.
- Hot or cold flushes.
- Increased frequency of dreams.
- Feelings of anger or any other negative emotion such as sadness.
- Abdominal pains.
- Feelings of peace and love.
- Increased tiredness.
- Diarrhea or frequent trips to the bathroom.
- Resurfacing of negative emotions attached to past events.
- Feelings of abandonment, being unsupported or lonely.
- Feelings of being unloved or not being good enough.
- Feelings of frustration or resentment.

You may undergo any of these experiences after a Reiki attunement and they are all slight, normal and temporary. Of course, it is always best to err on the side of caution and should you feel like you are experiencing anything that you believe to be a more serious health related issue, which is not connected to Reiki, it would be wise to have a professional healthcare provider check you out to be on the safe side.

When the vibration of your body increases during and after a Reiki attunement, the negative energies and blockages that you may be harboring within your body and mind will naturally be unblocked and will rise to the surface. While this can sometimes be uncomfortable and confusing, it plays a natural part in your healing process. You may also notice that you start to gravitate away from certain relationships and people, as often the cause of our energy blockages can be connected to the negative people in our lives. Keep in mind that your mind and body are going through a deep healing and aspects of your life will naturally change when your body and mind begin to vibrate at a different frequency, sometimes affecting the resonance you may once have had with other people in your life.

This is all a positive experience as you bring yourself to a new level of being and awareness. What serves you will remain and often the root cause of the stresses and negativity in your life will naturally become increasingly undesirable to you. You may experience none of the above, however keep it within your mind and awareness that when such things do surface, they do so for your highest and greatest good and have a reason for doing so. This is important to always remember. Whatever does happen after your attunement is for you *highest and greatest good only* and by the end of it, you will have shed your past skin and become a new improved version of your former self.

21-DAY SELF CARE AND REIKI TREATMENTS

During your 21-Day-Cleansing, it is recommended that you treat yourself with Reiki on a daily basis, preferably for an hour each day, or for as long as you can manage. By working on yourself daily during these 21-Days and beyond, you will help to raise your bodies vibrations and ensure your cleansing period is as pleasurable as possible. This will help to accelerate your bodies natural healing ability and will speed up the removal of negative energy blockages within your mind, body and Spirit.

One thing that is guaranteed after your Reiki attunement is positive change. So be aware that you may notice subtle and/or sudden changes to every aspect of your life, increasingly so as you complete higher degree attunements. As the high frequency Reiki energy enters and cleanses your body, it automatically breaks up any low vibration negativity. That includes any toxins, impurities and free-radicals you may have in your body. To help avoid any discomfort and to aid this healing process, drink sufficient amounts of water to help flush these toxins from your system. You may also notice that:

- Eating meat makes you feel tired or sick. Reducing your meat consumption or becoming vegetarian is not uncommon.
- Alcohol may make you feel sick or uncomfortable. Reducing your alcohol intake is another common occurrence following a Reiki attunement.
- You no longer feel the same pleasure smoking as you did prior to your attunement.
- Your taste-buds may change and foods and drink that you once enjoyed may no longer please your pallet.
- You may become aware of your life purpose and make significant changes to your life.

See this time as an opportunity to cleanse and heal your body and use Reiki on yourself every day, if possible. This will help keep you relaxed, stress free, energized, calm, and mentally focused and will help to alleviate any mental or emotional blockages that rise to the surface after your attunement. Try to avoid drinking alcohol and stimulants such as energy drinks, coffee or tea during this 21-Day period and drink plenty of water or herbal tea if you wish. Also give yourself a sufficient amount of sleep each night to aid this process. Experts recommend that we all have no less than six hours sleep per night and no more than eight. Seven hours is recommended to be the optimal amount of sleep to have each night. If you find yourself wanting to sleep more, listen to your body and do so.
Also try to stay relaxed during thid period as this will also be beneficial. Taking some time to soak in the bathtub with some added natural mineral salts, relaxing music

and a few candles at night will all help to keep your body and mind in a relaxed state of being.

Keeping a diary of your experiences during this 21-Day-Cleansing period can be an interesting thing to look back over in the future. Reminding you of the subtle or significant changes you have undergone as a result of receiving your Reiki attunements. As you complete higher level attunements in Reiki, you are gradually improving your connection to Source. This naturally opens you up more spiritually and increasing your awareness and realization of both your inner and outer worlds. Our consciousness's are linked, so as yours develops further, so too does your perception of the world, others and yourself.

Keep in mind to drink sufficient amounts of water to keep yourself well hydrated and remember, the thoughts you give energy to create the world as you see it.

CHAPTER 40
PREPARING FOR A REIKI ATTUNEMENT

❝ *When words are both true and kind, they can change our world.* **❞ – Buddha**

Before performing any of the Attunements, prepare your room and yourself first. A sacred space should be created in order to perform the sacred rituals of Reiki and one should always bring respect for the energies they are working with into all their energy workings. To clear the room and make your space sacred, perform the following steps:

- Have your client sit comfortably with hands in Gassho prayer position.
- With your own hands in Gassho position, state your intention and say a short prayer for your client, silently stating that you will be performing a Healing Attunement, Reiki I Attunement, Reiki II Attunement etc..
- Then place your hands in Reiji-ho, thumbs to your third eye Chakra, and call in your guides. Ask to be a clear and pure channel to receive the spirit of Reiki.
- Visualize a Choku Rei on each wall, the ceiling and the floor. Say its mantra three times as you draw each one.
- Now visualize the Tibetan Dai Ko Mio, the Usui Dai Ko Myo, Hon Sha Ze Sho Nen, Sei Heki, and Choku Rei, into the palms of your hands. Visualize a large Choku Rei down the front of your body and visualize a Choku Rei on each of your seven main Chakras, starting at the Root Chakra and finishing on the Crown Chakra, placing your hands over each Chakra as you do so.
- Now visualize/draw all six of the Reiki symbols, the previously mentioned symbols and the Fire Serpent symbol, in the center of the room, intending that the room be filled with the healing energy of each symbol.

Now you have created a sacred environment, you are ready to proceed with the Violet Breath technique. Once you have done this, you are ready to perform your Healing Attunement on your client, or any one of the Reiki Student Attunement levels, I, II, Reiki Master or Reiki Master Teacher.

- This completes the preparation for giving an attunement. -

CHAPTER 41
VIOLET BREATH – A.K.A DRAGON BREATH

❝If we could see the miracle of a single flower clearly, our whole life would change.❞ **– Buddha**

The Violet Breath technique is used to channel the Tibetan Dai Ko Mio into the heart of your client during a Healing attunement, or into the brain during a students initiation Attunement into Reiki. After preparing for an attunement, stand behind your client and place your hands upon their head to make an energetic connection. Then perform the Violet Breath as follows:

- Touch the tip of your tongue to the roof of your mouth and contract your Hui Yin, located at your perineum.
- Take a slow deep breath and visualize a bright white light from above entering your Crown Chakra and flowing through your tongue, down the front of your throat, chest, then stomach and looping over your Perineum and travelling back up your spine to your Crown Chakra. *(This is one loop of your bodies upper energy system)*
- Try to feel the energy as it loops around the body and continue this visualization until you can feel the energy build. *(**Tip**: the quicker you visualize the energy spinning around this loop, the more energy will be drawn into your body through the Crown)*
- Now when the energy is travelling up your spine the final time, visualize it going into your brain and spinning clockwise in a white mist. As this mist spins, imagine it quickly turning from white to blue, then to violet. You should now have a violet mist spinning clockwise in your head. Continue to visualize this spinning violet mist while performing the next step.
- Within this violet mist, at the center of your brain, draw the Tibetan Dai Ko Mio, however do not rotate it.

213

- Then gently blow and breathe the violet mist and the Tibetan Dai Ko Mio into the Crown Chakra of your client. Imagine both the violet mist and the Tibetan Dai Ko Mio penetrating your students brain and flowing down through the brain to the base of the skull.
- Remember to hold your tongue and Hui Yin in place for the duration of the technique.

- This completes the Violet Breath technique. -

CHAPTER 42
HEALING ATTUNEMENTS

❝ *He is able who thinks he is able.* ❞ **– Buddha**

The process of giving a Healing Attunement to a client is very similar to giving a student Reiki Attunement, with a few slight yet significant differences. The Healing Attunement is given for deep healing purposes and brings in a high vibration of energy to the session. However the Healing Attunement does not initiate a person into Reiki. This is because the Healing attunement does not open the energy pathways through the arms or the palm Chakras of your client, so they will be unable to channel Reiki themselves. Your client will receive a similar level of healing as a student attunement, however they will not be able to use the energy themselves without receiving that student attunement and the energy will dissipate from their body after a few days.

The most powerful way to deeply heal a client is to first use the Healing Attunement, followed by Psychic Surgery, then completed with a standard Reiki treatment. The healing is as flexible as Reiki itself, so it can also be used for the following:

- To empower goals – Your client may have negative thoughts, negative feelings, or deep rooted blockages that are preventing them from achieving the life they want. If your client is aware of the block, have them focus their attention on this negative blockage while you perform the Healing Attunement and this will help release the block from their body and energy field.
- You can also perform a Healing Attunement while having your client focus on this negative blockage, by giving it a shape, colour, texture etc., just as done during Psychic Surgery. This can be a psychologically empowering experience for your client that will stay with them long after their Reiki treatment has concluded.

As with everything, your own experimentation will yield its own results. The most capable healers are the ones that are willing to experiment and work on developing their practice and understanding of energy and its relationship with the body.

Prepare your space, perform your ritual and enter a receptive healing state in body and mind. Have your client seated with their feet flat on the floor, their spine straight and with their palms faced down on their legs. Your clients eyes should be closed. Perform the Healing Attunement as follows:

(Remember to first prepare your room & yourself to give the Healing Attunement beforehand, as previously mentioned)

Stand behind your client and perform the Healing Attunement as follows:

- Part One -

1. **Fire Serpent** - Now using your dominant hand, draw the Tibetan Fire Serpent over your client using your palm. Draw the top of the Fire Serpent a foot or so above your clients Crown Chakra, meander it down their spine, and coil its end at their root Chakra. All using your palm and remember to say the mantra, *"Fire Serpent"*, three times as you do so.
2. **Connect** – Place both your palms on top of your clients head and close your eyes. Meditate for a moment to achieve an energetic connection with your client.
3. **Violet Breath** – Touch the tip of your tongue to the roof of your mouth and contract your Hui Yin. Hold your Hui Yin and tongue in place for the duration of the Healing Attunement. Now perform the Violet Breath. Open your hands and exhale the Violet Breath into your clients Crown Chakra. Imagine the Violet colour and *Tibetan Dai Ko Mio* entering the crown of your client. Then place your dominant palm over their Crown and slowly motion the Dai Ko Mio down the back of their head, down their neck and to the Heart Chakra on their back.

Your non-dominant hand should stay on their head. As you do this, say *Dai Ko Mio* three times.

4. **Usui Dai Ko Myo** – Now draw the *Usui Dai Ko Myo* over your clients Crown, then slowly motion it slowly down to the Heart Chakra again, using your dominant hand. Saying *"Dai Ko Myo"* three times as you do so.

5. **Repeat** – Now repeat the previous step with *Hon Sha Ze Sho Nen*, *Sei Heki*, and *Choku Rei*.

Now move to stand in front of your client and proceed as follows:

- Part Two –

1. **Front symbols** – Draw the Tibetan Dai Ko Mio over the Crown Chakra. Say its mantra three times as your dominant hand slowly guides the energy and symbol down the third eye and throat till you reach the Heart Chakra.

2. **Repeat** – Now repeat the previous step with the Usui Dai Ko Myo, Hon Sha Ze Sho Nen, Sei Heki and Choku Rei. Guide each of these symbols from the Crown Chakra to the Heart Chakra with love and intention.

3. **Blowing with hands** – Take a big deep breath and with one continuous exhale, slowly blow from the Heart Chakra up to the Crown Chakra, back to the Heart Chakra and back to the Crown Chakra again. As you blow, use the palms of your hands to guide the energy into each Chakra, the Heart, the Throat, the Third Eye and Crown Chakra. On the last blow, from the Heart back to the Crown, stongly intend for all negative energies to be moved up your clients main energy pathway *(up their spine)* and out of their crown. Returning this negative energy to the Divine Source so it may be recycled.

Now move behind your client again and proceed as follows:

- Part Three –

1. **Affirmation -** Place your hands on your clients shoulders and look down through their Crown Chakra to their Heart Chakra, visualizing a pink ball of spinning light in their Heart Chakra. *(You can also visualize a gold, white or green ball instead of pink)* State a silent affirmation for your client, such as, *"I am looking deep into your Heart Chakra and talking direct to your subconscious and higher self. You have successfully received a deep Healing Attunement and have been blessed with love and healing light."* Repeat this three times.

2. **Sealing –** With your dominant hand over your clients Heart Chakra on their back, your non-dominant hand on their shoulder, with intention silently repeat the following three times, *"I seal in this healing energy with Divine love and light."* Do this while visualizing a Choku Rei over the back of their Heart Chakra to help seal in the energies.

3. **Blessing –** Place both your hands upon your clients shoulders with the feeling that you have both been blessed by this Healing Attunement. Say a short prayer asking that your client be blessed and healed by the Divine Source. Then with your fingers pointing to your own Heart Chakra with the back of your hands touching one another, release your tongue and Hui Yin as you exhale, intending that the releasing energy acts as a blessing for your client as you extend your hands outwards, as though you are about to give them a hug.

This completes the Healing Attunement. You can now perform your closing ritual and give thanks to your guides. Before you do so, have your student place their hands over their Heart Chakra and ask them to try and feel the energies that have just been channelled into them and when ready, to open their eyes.

- This completes the Healing Attunement. -

CHAPTER 43
REIKI I ATTUNEMENT

❝ *Your Heart contains the essence of your Spirit. You must open your heart in order to be truly free.* ❞ - **Ricky Mathieson**

(Prepare your room & yourself to give the Reiki I Attunement)

Stand behind your student and perform the Reiki I Attunement as follows:

- Part One -

1. **Fire Serpent** - Using your dominant hand, draw the Tibetan Fire Serpent over your students head using your palm. Draw the top curve of the Fire Serpent a foot or so above your students Crown Chakra, meander it down their spine, and coil its end at their root Chakra. Do so using your palm and remember to say the mantra, *"Fire Serpent"*, three times as you do so.
2. **Connect** – Place both your palms on top of your students head and close your eyes. Meditate for a moment to achieve an energetic connection with your student and proceed once you feel this connection.
3. **Violet Breath** – Touch the tip of your tongue to the roof of your mouth and contract your Hui Yin. Hold your Hui Yin and tongue in place for the duration of the attunement. Now perform the Violet Breath. Gently exhale the Violet Breath into your students Crown Chakra, imagining the Violet colour and *Tibetan Dai Ko Mio* entering the crown of your student. Then place your dominant palm over their Crown and slowly motion the Dai Ko Mio down the back of their head to the base of their skull. Where the spine meets the head. As you do this, say the mantra, *Dai Ko Mio,* three times.
4. **Usui Dai Ko Myo** – Now draw the *Usui Dai Ko Myo* over your students Crown, then slowly motion it down to

the base of the skull again, using your dominant hand. Say the mantra for this symbol, *"Dai Ko Myo"*, three times as you do so.

5. **Bring Students Hands To Crown** – Reach over and bring the students prayer clasped hands from their Heart Chakra, to the top of their head. Their hands should still be in prayer position with fingers pointing towards the ceiling, resting on top of their head.
6. **Hand Symbols** – While holding your students hands above their head with your non-dominant hand, visualize a Choku Rei in the air over your students fingertips. Then with your dominant hand, motion the Choku Rei down through the hands to the base of the skull, saying its mantra three times as you do so.
7. **Return Hands To Heart** – Now gently move your students prayer clasped hands from their head and return them to Gassho prayer position at their Heart Chakra.

Now move to stand in front of your student and proceed as follows:

- Part Two –

1. **Hand Symbols** – Take your students hands from Gassho prayer position and open them, so their palms are flat and facing the ceiling, and support them with your non-dominant hand. Now with your dominant hand, visualize a Choku Rei above their palms and motion it down into each of their palms. Silently say the mantra, Choku Rei, three times as you do so.
2. **Blowing on Students hands** – Bring the students hands together in Gassho prayer position and return them to their Heart Chakra. Holding their hands between your palms, take a deep breath and with one continuous exhale, slowly blow over their hands, down to their Root Chakra, up to their Crown Chakra, back down over their

hands to the Root Chakra, and back up ending at their hands.

Now move behind your client again and proceed as follows:

- Part Three –

1. **Affirmation** - Place your hands on your clients shoulders and look down through their Crown Chakra to their Root Chakra, visualizing a red ball of spinning light in their Root Chakra. State a silent affirmation for your client, such as, *"I am looking deep into your Root Chakra and talking direct to your subconscious and higher self. You have successfully received the Reiki I Attunement and have been blessed with love and healing light."* Repeat this affirmation for your client three times.
2. **Sealing** – Now visualize a Choku Rei on each of your thumbs and place your two thumbs at the base of your students skull. With wholehearted intention, silently repeat the following three times, *"I seal in this attunement with Divine love and light."*
3. **Blessing** – Place both your hands upon your clients shoulders with the feeling that you have both been blessed by this Reiki I Attunement. Say a short prayer asking that your client be blessed and healed. Then with your fingers pointing to your own Heart Chakra, the backs of your hands touching one another, release your tongue and Hui Yin as you exhale, intending that the releasing energy acts as a blessing for your client as you extend your hands and arms outwards, as though you are about to give them a hug.

This completes the Reiki I Practitioner Attunement. You can now perform your closing ritual and give thanks to the guides you called upon for assistance. Before you do so however, have your student place both of their hands over their Heart Chakra and ask them to try and feel the energies they have just been attuned to and when ready, to open their eyes.

- This completes the Reiki I Attunement. –

Although many of your students may not feel any sensations in their body during their attunement, most will feel a deep sense of relaxation and peace. This can be a good time for your student to continue to meditate once you have finished the attunement. It's not uncommon for some students to remain in meditation for 5 to 10 minutes, or longer, after you have concluded the attunement. It should be made clear to your students before you begin that they are welcome to continue meditating once you've finished the attunement process. This is a deeply special and healing moment in your students life and you should give them the freedom to enjoy their experience to the fullest.

CHAPTER 44
REIKI II ATTUNEMENT

(Prepare your room & yourself to give the Reiki II Attunement)

Stand behind your student and perform the Reiki II Attunement as follows:

- Part One -

1. **Fire Serpent** - Now using your dominant hand, draw the Tibetan Fire Serpent over your students head using your palm. Draw the top curve of the Fire Serpent a foot or so above your students Crown Chakra, meander it down their spine, and coil its end at their root Chakra. Do so using your palm and remember to say the mantra, *"Fire Serpent"*, three times as you do so.

2. **Connect** – Next place both your palms on top of your students head and close your eyes. Meditate for a moment to achieve an energetic connection with your student and proceed once you feel this connection.

3. **Violet Breath** – Now touch the tip of your tongue to the roof of your mouth and contract your Hui Yin at your perineum. Hold your Hui Yin and tongue in place for the duration of the attunement. Now perform the Violet Breath technique. Open your hands and exhale the Violet Breath into your students Crown Chakra, imagining the Violet colour and *Tibetan Dai Ko Mio* entering the crown of your student. Then place your dominant palm over their Crown and slowly motion the Dai Ko Mio down the back of their head to the base of their skull, where the spine meets the head. As you do this, say *Dai Ko Mio* three times.

4. **Usui Dai Ko Myo** – Now draw the *Usui Dai Ko Myo* over your students Crown, then slowly motion it down to the base of the skull again using your dominant hand. Say *"Dai Ko Myo"* three times as you do this.

5. **Bring Students Hands To Crown** – Reach over and bring the students prayer clasped hands from their Heart Chakra, to the top of their head. Your students hands should still be in prayer position with their fingers pointing towards the ceiling when you rest their hands on top of their head.

6. **Hand Symbols** – While holding your students hands above their head with your non-dominant hand, visualize a Choku Rei in the air over your students fingertips. Then with your dominant hand, motion the Choku Rei down through the hands to the base of the skull, and say its mantra three times as you do so. Do the same with Hon Sha Ze Sho Nen and Sei Heki.

7. **Return Hands To Heart** – Now gently move your students prayer clasped hands from their head and back into Gassho position at their Heart Chakra.

Now move to stand in front of your student and proceed as follows:

- Part Two –

1. **Hand Symbols** – Take your students hands from Gassho position and open them so their palms are flat and facing the ceiling and support them with your non-dominant hand. Now with your dominant hand, visualize a Choku Rei above their palms and motion it down into each of their palms. Silently say its mantra as you do so. Do the same with Hon Sha Ze Sho Nen and Sei Heki.

2. **Blowing on Students hands** – Bring your students hands together in Gassho prayer position once again and return their hands to their Heart Chakra. Hold their hands between your palms, take a deep breath and with one slow, continuous exhale, slowly blow over their hands, down to their Root Chakra, up to their Crown Chakra, back down over their hands to their Root Chakra, and back up ending at their hands.

224

Now move behind your client again and proceed as follows:

- Part Three –

1. **Affirmation** - Place your hands on your clients shoulders and look down through their Crown Chakra to their Root Chakra while visualizing a red ball of spinning light in their Root Chakra. State a silent affirmation for your client, such as, *"I am looking deep into your Root Chakra and talking direct to your subconscious and higher self. You have successfully received the Reiki II Attunement and have been blessed with love and healing light."* Repeat this three times.

2. **Sealing** – Now visualize a Choku Rei on each of your thumbs and place your two thumbs at the base of your students skull. With intention, silently repeat the following three times, *"I seal in this attunement with Divine love and light."*

3. **Blessing** – Place both your hands upon your clients shoulders with the feeling that you have both been blessed by this Reiki II Attunement. Say a short prayer asking that your client be blessed and healed. Then with your fingers pointing to your own Heart Chakra, the backs of your hands touching one another, release your tongue and Hui Yin as you exhale, intending that the releasing energy acts as a blessing for your client as you extend your hands and arms outwards, as though you are about to give them a hug.

This completes the Reiki II Attunement. You can now perform your closing ritual and give thanks to your guides. Before you do so, have your student place their hands over their Heart Chakra and ask them to try and feel the energies they have just been attuned to and when ready, to open their eyes.

- This completes the Reiki II Attunement. -

CHAPTER 45
REIKI III – MASTER PRACTITIONER ATTUNEMENT

(Prepare your room & yourself to give the Reiki III Master-Attunement)

Stand behind your student and perform the Reiki Master Attunement as follows:

- Part One -

1. **Fire Serpent** - Now using your dominant hand, draw the Tibetan Fire Serpent over your students head using your palm. Draw the top curve of the Fire Serpent a foot or so above your students Crown Chakra, meander it down their spine, and coil its end at their root Chakra. Do so using your palm and remember to say the mantra, *"Fire Serpent"*, three times as you do so.

2. **Connect** – Then place both your palms on top of your students head and close your eyes. Meditate for a moment to achieve an energetic connection with your student and proceed once you feel this connection.

3. **Violet Breath** – Touch the tip of your tongue to the roof of your mouth and contract your Hui Yin at your perineum. Hold your Hui Yin and tongue in place for the duration of the attunement. Now perform the Violet Breath. Open your hands and slowly exhale the Violet Breath into your students Crown Chakra and imagine the Violet colour and *Tibetan Dai Ko Mio* entering the crown of your student. Then place your dominant palm over their Crown and slowly motion the Dai Ko Mio down the back of their head to the base of their skull. Where the spine meets the head. As you do this, say *Dai Ko Mio* three times.

4. **Bring Students Hands To Crown** – Reach over and bring the students prayer clasped hands from their Heart Chakra to the top of their head. Your student should

227

still have their hands in prayer position with their fingers pointing towards the ceiling when you rest their hands on top of their head.

5. **Hand Symbols** – While holding your students hands above their head with your non-dominant hand, visualize the *Usui Dai Ko Myo* over your students fingertips, then slowly motion it down through their hands, through their skull and brain and to the base of their skull using your dominant hand. Say the mantra, *"Dai Ko Myo"* three times as you do so. Do the same with Choku Rei, Hon Sha Ze Sho Nen and Sei Heki.

6. **Return Hands To Heart** – Now gently move your students prayer clasped hands from their head and back into Gassho prayer position at their Heart Chakra.

Now move to stand in front of your student and proceed as follows:

- Part Two –

1. **Hand Symbols** – Now take your students hands from Gassho prayer position and open them, so their palms are flat and facing the ceiling, and support them with your non-dominant hand. Now using your dominant hand, visualize the Usui Dai Ko Myo above their palms and motion it down into each of their palms. Silently say the *Dai Ko Myo* mantra as you do so. Continue and do the same with Choku Rei, Hon Sha Ze Sho Nen and Sei Heki.

2. **Blowing on Students hands** – Bring the students hands together in Gassho prayer position and return them to their Heart Chakra. Hold their hands between your palms and take a deep breath and with one slow, continuous exhale, slowly blow over their hands, down to their Root Chakra, up to their Crown Chakra, back down over their hands to the Root Chakra, and back up ending at their hands.

Now move behind your client again and proceed as follows:

- Part Three –

1. **Affirmation** - Place your hands on your clients shoulders and look down through their Crown Chakra to their Root Chakra and visualize a red ball of spinning light in their Root Chakra. State a silent affirmation for your client, such as, *"I am looking deep into your Root Chakra and talking direct to your subconscious and higher self. You have successfully received the Reiki Master Attunement and have been blessed with love and healing light."* Repeat this three times.

2. **Sealing** – Now visualize a Choku Rei on each of your thumbs and place your two thumbs at the base of your students skull. With intention, silently repeat the following three times, *"I seal in this attunement with Divine love and light."*

3. **Blessing** – Place both your hands upon your clients shoulders with the feeling that you have both been blessed by this Reiki Master Attunement. Say a short prayer asking that your client be blessed and healed. Then with your fingers pointing to your own Heart Chakra, the backs of your hands touching one another, release your tongue and Hui Yin as you exhale, intending that the releasing energy acts as a blessing for your client as you extend your hands and arms outwards, as though you are about to give them a hug.

This completes the Reiki Master Practitioner Attunement. You can now perform your closing ritual and give thanks to your guides. Before you do so, have your student place their hands over their Heart Chakra and ask them to try and feel the energies they have just been attuned to and when ready, to open their eyes.

- This completes the Master Practitioner Attunement. -

CHAPTER 46
MASTER-TEACHER ATTUNEMENT

The Master-Teacher attunement gives students the ability to attune others to Reiki. All six Reiki symbols are put into the hands, when hands are in Gassho on top of the students head and when their palms are held in front of their Heart Chakra.

(Prepare your room & yourself to give the Reiki Master-Teacher Attunement.)

Stand behind your student and perform the Reiki Master-Teacher Attunement as follows:

- Part One -

1. **Fire Serpent** - Now using your dominant hand, draw the Tibetan Fire Serpent over your students head using your palm. Draw the top curve of the Fire Serpent a foot or so above your students Crown Chakra, meander it down their spine, and coil its end at their root Chakra. Do so using your palm and remember to say the mantra, *"Fire Serpent"*, three times as you do so.
2. **Connect** – Place both your palms on top of your students head and close your eyes. Meditate for a moment to achieve an energetic connection with your student.
3. **Bring Students Hands To Crown** – Reach over and bring the students prayer clasped hands from their Heart Chakra to the top of their head. Your students hands should still be in prayer position with their fingers pointing towards the ceiling, hands resting on top of their head.
4. **Violet Breath** – Touch the tip of your tongue to the roof of your mouth and contract your Hui Yin. Hold your Hui Yin and tongue in place for the duration of the attunement. Now perform the Violet Breath. Open your hands and exhale the Violet Breath through your students hands, imaging the Tibetan Dai Ko Mio travelling through

their hands into their Crown Chakra. Then use your dominant palm and slowly motion the Dai Ko Mio down the back of their head to the base of their skull where the spine meets the head. As you do this, silently say the *Dai Ko Mio* mantra three times.

5. **Hand Symbols** – While holding your students hands above their head with your non-dominant hand, visualize the Tibetan Fire Serpent in the air over your students hands. Then with your dominant hand, motion the Fire Serpent down through the hands to the base of the skull and say its mantra three times as you do so. Repeat this step with the Usui Dai Ko Myo, Hon Sha Ze Sho Nen, Sei Heki and Choku Rei.

6. **Return Hands To Heart** – Now gently move your students prayer clasped hands from their head and back into Gassho position at their Heart Chakra.

Now move to stand in front of your student and proceed as follows:

- Part Two –

1. **Hand Symbols** – Take your students hands from Gassho position and open them, so their palms are flat and facing the ceiling, and support them with your non-dominant hand. Now with your dominant hand, visualize the Tibetan Dai Ko Mio above their palms and motion it down into each one. Silently say its mantra as you do so. Do the same with the Fire Serpent, the Usui Dai Ko Myo, Hon Sha Ze Sho Nen, Sei Heki and Choku Rei.

2. **Blowing on Students hands** – Bring the students hands together in Gassho prayer position and return them to their Heart Chakra. Hold your students hands between your palms, take a deep breath and with one continuous exhale, slowly blow over their hands, down to their Root Chakra, up to their Crown Chakra, back down over their hands to the Root Chakra, and back up ending at their hands.

Now move behind your client again and proceed as follows:

- Part Three –

1. **Affirmation** - Place your hands on your clients shoulders and look down through their Crown Chakra to their Root Chakra, visualizing a red ball of spinning light in their Root Chakra. State a silent affirmation for your client, such as, *"I am looking deep into your Root Chakra and talking direct to your subconscious and higher self. You have successfully received the Reiki Master-Teacher Attunement and have been blessed with love and healing light."* Repeat this three times.

2. **Sealing** – Now visualize a Choku Rei on each of your thumbs and place your two thumbs at the base of your students skull. With intention, silently repeat the following three times, *"I seal in this attunement with Divine love and light."*

3. **Blessing** – Place both your hands upon your clients shoulders with the feeling that you have both been blessed by this Reiki Master-Teacher Attunement. Say a short prayer asking that your client be blessed and healed. Then with your fingers pointing to your own Heart Chakra, the backs of your hands touching one another, release your tongue and Hui Yin as you exhale, intending that the releasing energy acts as a blessing for your client as you extend your hands and arms outwards, as though you are about to give them a hug.

This completes the Reiki Master-Teacher Attunement. You can now perform your closing ritual and give thanks to your guides. Before you do so, have your student place their hands over their Heart Chakra and ask them to try and feel the energies they have just been attuned to and when ready, to open their eyes.

- This completes the Master-Teacher Attunement. -

CHAPTER 47
DISTANCE ATTUNEMENTS & ATTUNING ONESELF

DISTANCE ATTUNEMENTS

Just as one can give a Reiki treatment at a distance, so too can one give a Reiki Attunement for an absent client with the same result as though that client was in your presence and receiving a hands-on attunement. You should be aware however, that distance attunements are not recognized by Reiki Regulatory Organisations and those students will not qualify for insurance if attunements have not been done in person.

To obtain insurance and join any of the UK's Reiki Regulatory Organisations, one must have received their Reiki Attunements in person. Therefore it's recommended that your students are present with you during your class and attunements. This also ensures you can properly guide your students should they experience any reactions during the attunement process. As safe as Reiki is, it can still cause your student to become anxious or fearful if they don't understand the changes they may experience as a result of the attunement process and Reiki is about removing negative energy blockages, not creating them.

If you are sending a Distance Reiki Attunement, call your student and have them sit comfortably on a chair as you perform the Reiki Attunement. Then state your intention to send whichever Reiki Attunement you wish to your absent student. To perform the attunement, you can use a teddy bear or pillow to act as a physical replacement for your absent student. Or you can use a chair and simply visualize the student sitting on the chair as you perform the attunement.

Before you begin the attunement, it is important to bridge a connection with your absent student. To do so, remember to use the distance symbol, Hon Sha Ze Sho Nen, before passing the attunement. State your students name three times and intend that the attunement will pass over distance to your student. Spend a minute or so establishing an energetic connection with your student before beginning the attunement process. When you have done so, you can then proceed with the normal steps for whatever attunement level you are passing.

ATTUNING YOURSELF

Once you have reached Master-Teacher level in Reiki you are able to pass attunements to yourself as well as others. Giving yourself regular self-attunements to Master-Teacher level is an effective way of cleansing your mind, body and energy field of any undesirable negative energy that may have clung to your being. Attuning yourself regularly will help to strengthen your connection to Reiki and you can attune yourself as many times as you desire, even every day if you so wish. Use the same distance attunement method described previously to pass a self-attunement and remember to use the distance symbol and state your intention to attune yourself.

You can use a teddy bear or pillow to perform a self-attunement or you can use a chair and imagine yourself to be sitting in it. An alternative to using a teddy or pillow is to use any other point of focus or use just your mind. Start the attunement process by sitting in a chair and grounding yourself, then call in your guides and set your intention to pass a self-distance attunement to yourself. Then meditate for a moment to establish your connection with Reiki. Then stand up from your chair and walk to the back of it and imagine your energy body to be left sitting in the chair. Then proceed to perform the attunement on this invisible image of yourself. When you are finished, sit back in the chair and back into your energy body and meditate for a while to feel the presence of the attunement energies.

Self-attunements can be done every day if you wish as there is no limit to how many times you can be attuned.

PART 5:

TEACHING REIKI

"Just as treasures are uncovered from the earth, so virtue appears from good deeds, and wisdom appears from a pure and peaceful mind. To walk safely through the maze of human life, one needs the light of wisdom and the guidance of virtue."
– Buddha

CHAPTER 48
THE ROLE OF A REIKI MASTER

66 *Meeting new people gives us an opportunity for fresh understanding and new growth. However no matter what Masters may enter your life and no matter what you may learn from them, remember that you are already a Master of your own life. And with that mastery, you can give back just as much value as is offered to you. Your struggles in life, your defeats, your sufferings, your losses and your tears have all helped make you the beautiful person you have become. Share these experiences because despite always having something to learn in life, we each always have something to give.* **99** - **Ricky Mathieson**

Being a Reiki Master-Teacher is an important position to be in and one should conduct themselves in a responsible manner. Reiki is a sacred spiritual practice that must have your deepest respect if one is to experience its deeper values. Not only is a Reiki Master-Teacher expected to be in control of the direction of their own life, they are expected to live, act, behave and teach their students in such a way as to bring out the very best in those students.

A Reiki Master-Teacher is expected to live their life in accordance with the Reiki Principles and be constantly working on their own awareness and spiritual development. If a Reiki Master has stopped upon the path towards full spiritual enlightenment they have become stagnant and we all must continually strive to challenge ourselves in order to create positive change and to fulfill the unique purpose of our lives.

Keep in mind that what you say and how you teach your students will have a profound effect upon how Reiki affects their lives and how this healing art is carried forward and taught in the future. Words are powerful and every word holds its own energy and that energy can either inspire your students or discourage them. With this in mind, always choose your words as carefully as you should choose your own thoughts.

Unconditional love, compassion, a non-judgmental nature, humility, kindness, courage, strength and encouragement are the minimum qualities one should strive to achieve. It would be expected for you to continue upon your path of self-growth and personal development in your quest to understand the many wonders of Reiki and life itself. As a Reiki Teacher, you should be living a life of Reiki and your life should set a good example for your students.

One should work on removing their competitive nature and should always be willing to help students reach their maximum potential. Even if that means your student sets up their own Reiki teaching business in your own area. The importance of humanity re-connecting with their spiritual roots and heritage is infinitely more important than a bank balance and by acting with the best of intentions, Reiki will provide for you in return.

When a Reiki Teacher gifts an attunement to a student, they have created a permanent bond between master and student that should be maintained and the up-most respect should be shown to all students who cross your path. Unlike any other type of tutorship, a Reiki Master is expected to offer advice and assistance to their students from the attunement onwards and be there to help guide students on their spiritual path. It is a commitment like no other. As a Reiki Master-Teacher, you are expected to be proficient and knowledgeable with all the information and techniques listed in this manual, at the very least, and should have a working knowledge of the symbols, their associated energies and what can be done with them.

Reiki must be experienced first-hand by your students and is not something that can be fully understood on an intellectual basis. Ensuring your classes involve plenty of practical, hands-on experience is important for your students to give them the necessary confidence in their new found abilities and to strengthen their belief in themselves. It is very helpful for your students, and for your business, to host a monthly Reiki share, where attuned students and potential future students can gather and practice Reiki techniques on one another. This will refine your students energy and help keep them balanced, which makes sure they are in the best position for developing themselves and helping and healing others.

Under no circumstance should a Reiki Teacher use their position to wield power or control over their students and should in no way abuse their power and manipulate those around them. Free will is a vital component for all individuals and you should encourage your students to make use of their own power and guidance and allow them the freedom to make their own choices and mistakes. It is not the job of a Reiki Master to change someone's life. It's their job to empower and guide individuals towards learning how to change their own lives. As you truly empower others, the Spirit of Reiki will truly empower you in return, for you, humanity and the Divine are one.

A Reiki Master will soon come to realize that Reiki offers us far more than the simple ability to heal oneself and others. It gives us the knowledge, tools and ability to help people change their lives and the wider world by opening our consciousness and awareness to what the human mind and heart is truly capable of. Our ability to heal ourselves, others and to determine our future experiences at will is the reality we each hold within ourselves. The power resting inside of us is far more potent than any of us have ever been led to believe and it's important that we do not interfere with or limit our power by imposing unfounded earthly beliefs, perceptions and pre-conceptions upon ourselves regarding what we think we are capable of.

Whatever you think you are capable of is the self-limiting reality you create for yourself. Whereas the real reality is that our true capabilities exist way beyond our intellectual means to understand them. Remember to keep an open mind with everything and a truly opened mind is a mind that is free of *all* thinking and belief. It's in this place of solitude and emptiness that you will find and connect to the power resting within and around you. Stop telling yourself what to believe and just be.

While being true, genuine and honest to your students is paramount, so is your ability to not be used and manipulated yourself. Naturally, you will come across individual students that come to expect more of you and you will experience needy students who expect an unreasonable amount of time, focus or energy from you. In such circumstances, it is important that you remain respectful, professional, kind, and strong in your dealings and don't allow yourself to be manipulated.

At the same time however, you must be able to use this opportunity to empower your students. One ill thought sentence can have a long lasting detrimental effect upon whom it is directed at so you should always choose your words carefully. However being kind does not mean bending to the every wish and desire of your students. It means treating them accordingly and being kind but stern if necessary. Remember, it's not your job to change your students lives, it's theirs. Your only job is to awaken and guide them towards their power. Doing everything for your students takes them away from their power center and contributes towards creating a relationship between you both that is based upon one way giving and dependency. Don't go on the defensive with any of your students who may expect more from you. Instead take this neediness and transform it into something positive that empowers your student, rather than creates a relationship based upon dependency.

When in need of guidance yourself, surrender and place your complete trust in the Spirit of Reiki and meditate on what direction to take in any given situation. When guidance is called upon with a pure and clear heart, the answers are always sure to follow. The only thing that stands in the way of knowing those answers is your awareness, however as you continue to work upon opening yourself further to the Divine Source, your awareness improves at the same time.

Remember, you already have valuable life experiences that could help improve the lives of others, so there is no time to teach like the present. Through teaching, you will deepen your connection to Reiki and will improve your understanding and awareness of your true nature through direct first-hand experience. You will meet many different people from all walks of life when teaching Reiki and in many instances these people can offer you valuable insight into your own life. With an unwavering belief in the magic of Reiki, we ensure we attract only what is best for us into our lives and you will develop a deep satisfaction in seeing your students gain confidence and self-belief in themselves as you help them grow into the powerful beings they all truly are. As their guide it is your job to help point the way, but know that you will never be alone and the Love, Light and energy of the Divine Source will be with you and guiding you at every moment, regardless of whether you are aware of this guidance or not.

CHAPTER 49
TEACHING YOUR OWN REIKI CLASSES

66 *Do not overrate what you have received nor envy others. He who envies others does not obtain peace of mind.* 99 **– Buddha**

Teaching your own Reiki classes can be a very rewarding experience, for your students as well as your own spiritual development. While your Reiki classes are flexible, in that you can pick and choose what topics to cover and which techniques to practise on the day, there are a few necessary basics that you should include in your teaching schedule.

Reiki 1st Degree

- The history of Reiki
- The Original Reiki Ideals
- Your Usui Reiki-Master lineage
- What Reiki is, its benefits and what it can be used for
- The Professional Ethics of Reiki
- Explaining the attunement process
- Understanding the symbols, how they work, how to activate them and when to use them
- The Importance of the Reiki Ideals and how they prepare ones mind to be a pure and clear channel
- Explaining the 21-day-cleansing and what each student could experience after their attunement
- The Reiki hand positions for giving treatments and the hand positions for giving self-treatments
- The Three Pillars of Reiki, what each one does and why they are performed
- Kenyoku Dry Bathing
- Hatsurei-ho Reiki Shower Technique
- The 7 main Chakras, their colours and their purpose
- Psychic Protection Techniques

- The Sacred Smudging Ceremony

Reiki 2ˢᵗ Degree

- Detailed explanation of the two new symbols
- How to use each symbol correctly and how to further empower each one
- How to empower goals and desires using Reiki
- How to perform distance healing treatments
- What each student may experience with this more emotional attunement
- Byosen Scanning
- Joshin Kokyu-ho Tan Den Breathing
- Jacki-Kiri Joka-ho Negative Energy Cleansing Method
- The law and legalities
- Any quotes or stories that are relevant to developing your students mind

Reiki Master-Practitioner

- Psychic Surgery
- The Master Symbol, what it does and how to use it
- Dai Ko Myo Moving Meditation
- Using the Tibetan Antahkarana
- Creating and using a Reiki Crystal Grid
- Reiki Master Meditation
- The Hui Yin and understanding and controlling energy flow

Reiki Master-Teacher

- How to perform a Reiju Empowerment
- How to perform a healing attunement
- How to perform the Violet Breath
- Preparations to make before each attunement
- How to perform each Reiki Attunement, 1ˢᵗ, 2ⁿᵈ, Master, and Master-Teacher

The previously suggested teaching schedules are the bare minimum knowledge base you should include in each of your Reiki classes. It can also be a good idea to include any knowledge and techniques in your teachings and manual that you think could be valuable for your students. You are the teacher and what you bring to your students should have your own personal touch, based upon your own relative life experiences with Reiki. You will find that you attract the students that are in resonance with your teaching style and experience of life, so your method of teaching will suit some people more than others. Being true to yourself is more important than being true to anyone else, so feel what works for you best and let your uniqueness shine through your teaching.

Remember an important point when teaching Reiki. *"A good teacher shows a student where to look. But does not tell them what to see."* It is both wise and best for your students to learn Reiki without too much personal belief and influence from yourself. Unless you feel it is valid and relevant to the practice of Reiki or may be of use to your students. Follow your heart and when in doubt, ask for guidance from the Divine Source while in meditation. As you help to guide others towards their true nature and help empower those around you, so too will guidance and progress be returned to you.

The importance of opening just one mind to its true nature can not be understated. When you help just one individual connect with their higher consciousness, this has a significant effect upon, not only that individual person but, all those people around them and the generations that follow. Every human being creates a reflection upon those around them as well as upon the very fabric of society itself. So it's important to be aware that when you spread Reiki to the wider world, it will have positive and far reaching effects that you may not be aware of. And when one casts the stone of positive change into the still waters, its ripples travel far and wide and return to you in time.

247

CHAPTER 50
REIKI STUDENT MANUAL

❝ *Work out your own salvation. Do not depend on others.* ❞ – **Buddha**

Whether you decide to teach Reiki levels one through to Master-Teacher level in three days or the more common five days, you will only have the time to cover the bare basics. There will be techniques that you will not have the time to teach at each level and these time restrictions may stop you teaching each topic in more depth. Because of this, the importance of writing up a good Reiki Students Manual is paramount to help aid the understanding and development of your students.

Your Reiki classes involve opening the Crown Chakra of your students *(connecting them to the Reiki energy)* and giving them sufficient time to practise and experience the energies themselves through the various techniques you teach in class. Including plenty of hands-on practise time for your students is important to help build their confidence in their new found abilities. Your Reiki Manual on the other hand, should give your students a detailed, in-depth account of what you covered in class and those techniques you didn't have time to teach.

You should also include what further steps one may take into Reiki and what can be achieved with it. Your first Reiki class, for Reiki 1st Degree, provides the perfect opportunity for writing a manual that prepares your students mind in the most productive way possible. Reiki works through the mind as well as the heart and all the rituals and techniques are designed to help students experience the Reiki energy productively. However it all comes down to how well mentally, emotionally, and physically your students are prepared, as well as what knowledge of Reiki you send them away with. Including a *recommended reading* section at the end of your manuals, which lists the valuable Reiki related books you have read, will offer your students much wisdom and guidance for their journey ahead.

As a teacher, you should make the most of this opportunity and keep in mind that the service you offer your students will be judged upon your Reiki Students Manual, as much as your energy and the class tuition itself. Your Reiki manual should be viewed as your training tool, your business card and your advertisement. Your student manual will create an avenue for future students to cross paths with you and hire your services, so you want it to be an accurate reflection of your skills and expertise.

You are welcome to supply your students with a bought copy of *'The Reiki Teachers Guidebook'* should you wish to. However it would be best to work towards writing your own students manual, so that your training manual is more in resonance with your own beliefs, practices and teaching style.

CHAPTER 51
CLASS OUTLINES

❝ *Words project your thoughts and intentions and create your reality. Peace of mind does not depend upon who or what you are. It relies solely upon what you think.* ❞ **– Ricky Mathieson**

How you plan the structure of your Reiki classes will depend upon how you wish to teach. You will have your own unique life experiences that could be helpful to your students and you may wish to include relevant aspects of these into your teaching manuals. Also, you will need to decide if you wish to teach Reiki as you have been taught, or if you wish to teach it differently. Personally, I teach Reiki 1st and 2nd Degree in one day, Master Practitioner in one day and Master-Teacher level in one day. However it is more common to spread Reiki I & II over two days and to teach Reiki Master-Teacher over two days also. Your priorities, the amount of content you wish to teach and the time available to practise each of the techniques you teach in class will all have a bearing upon how you structure your tuition.

Before your students arrive for their Reiki class, it is important that you create a suitable space for working with the Reiki energies. Cleanse your room/home using the smudging technique to remove negative energies and make the space sacred. Then protect your room/home by performing the *"Preparing For An Attunement"* ritual, by putting all six Usui symbols in your palms and then the middle of the room and intend that the energy of each symbol fills the room with love, light and healing energy.

As an example, the class outlines for my Reiki classes are as follows:

REIKI 1ST & 2ND DEGREE CLASSES
Taught in a one day class *(usually taught over two days)*

This is more taxing emotionally, mentally and spiritually, however it significantly raises ones ability to deal with the negative energy blockages that are released as a result. Over-emphasizing to your students the importance of regular self-treatments and working on ones own mental, emotional and physical well-being would be advised, especially during the 21-day cleansing period.

Suggested class time: 9am - 4pm **or** 10am – 5pm

Morning Session: Reiki 1st Degree

1. **Agenda For The Day** – Discuss with your students what the agenda for the day is, mentioning all the points listed in the morning and afternoon class.
2. **Students Talk** – To help break the ice and create group bonding, ask your students to mention why they are doing Reiki & what they hope to achieve from it.
3. **What is Reiki** – Describe what Reiki is, what it does and the nature of how it works
4. **How Attunements Work** – Explain the attunement process, what you will be doing, what your students will be required to do and how the attunement process works.
5. **21-Day-Cleansing Process** – Tell your students what they can expect after each attunement level.
6. **History & Origins of Reiki** – Cover the history of Reiki, its founder, its origins, and how it has spread and developed throughout the world since ancient times.
7. **What Reiki Can Be Used For** – Talk about all the things Reiki can be used for and in what limited situations Reiki should not be used.
8. **Gift of 1st Symbol** – Draw the symbol for your students and have them practise drawing it. (*read the symbol explanantion from this manual*)
9. **Give 1st Level Attunement** (*explain it first*) – Reiterate to your students where to place their hands and how you will direct their hands during the attunement process.

- **SHORT BREAK FOR 15 MINS -**

10. **How To Self-Cleanse Before & After A Treatment** – Have each student perform the Kenyoku Dry Bathing Technique. Explain the importance of self-cleansing before and after a treatment.

11. **The Reiki Principles** – Why they are important for self-development and how they prepare ones mind and help improve ones Reiki channelling abilities.

12. **Hand Positions Used** – Explain for self-treatments and treating others, whether seated or lying down.

13. **How To Activate The Symbols** – Explain the various ways your students can activate the Reiki symbols for giving treatments.

14. **Perform A Short Treatment** – Pair up your students and have them experience the energy of Choku Rei during a short treatment using the desired hand positions.

- GO FOR LUNCH –

Afternoon Session 2nd Degree

1. **Ethics of Reiki** – Always ask your clients permission before giving them Reiki and mention the importance of free will as being vital to a persons personal growth and development. Also remember to briefly reinforce the importance of practitioner/client confidentiality.

2. **3 Pillars of Reiki, Gassho, Reiji-Ho, Chiryo-ho** – Properly describe the purpose behind the three pillars of Reiki and how to perform each one.

3. **Gift Of Two 2nd Degree Symbols** – Have students practise drawing and memorizing how they are drawn.

4. **Explain 2nd Degree Symbols** – What they can be used for and how to power them up with Choku Rei. *(Read explanations for symbols out of this manual)*

5. **Give 2nd Degree Attunement** – Reiterate to your students where to place their hands and how you will direct their hands during the attunement process.

6. **Byosen Scanning** – Explain what to do, why to do it and what sensations your students might feel when scanning.

253

7. **Guided Meditation** *(optional)* – Perform a guided meditation for your students that incorporate the three symbols you have taught them into the visualisation. (*See resources section for example)*
8. **Students Perform A 20-Minute Reiki Treatment** – Split your students into groups and have them practise giving a treatment using the various hand positions and symbols and explain what sensations they could experience. Have them experiment with Byosen Scanning at this time.
9. **How To Use The Distance Symbol** – Have students perform a distance healing using a teddy bear, pillow, or just by thought and intention alone.
10. **Empowering goals and desires with Reiki** – Have your students write their goals on a piece of paper, write their name upon it, draw all three symbols on the paper, and perform a distance healing on it. Tell them to carry the piece of paper with them everywhere they go so it absorbs their energy constantly and Reiki it every day to maintain the highest energy levels possible.
11. **Joshin Kokyu-Ho – Tan Den breathing technique** – Have your students perform this exercise so they can experience how Reiki flows by thought and intention.
12. **Hatsurei-Ho** – have students perform the Reiki shower technique.

REIKI MASTER-PRACTITIONER CLASSES
Taught in a one day class *(usually taught in a one day class)*

Suggested class time: 9am - 4pm **or** 10am – 5pm
Morning Session:

1. **Agenda For The Day** – Discuss with your students what the agenda for the day is, mentioning all the points listed in the morning and afternoon class.
2. **Students Talk** – To help break the ice and create group bonding, ask your students to mention why they are doing Reiki & what they hope to achieve from it.
3. **Gift Of The Master Symbol** – Draw the Master Symbol for students and have them practise drawing it until memorized.
4. **Explanation Of The Master Symbol** – Read from the manual the nature of the Master Symbol and what it can be used for.
5. **How Attunements Work** – Explain the attunement process, what you will be doing, what your students will be required to do and how the attunement process works.
6. **21-Day-Cleansing Process** – Tell your students what they can expect after the Master Attunement.
7. **Give Master Attunement** – Give the Master Attunement to each of your students.
8. **Dai Ko Myo Moving Meditation** – Explain the Dai Ko Myo Moving Meditation and have the whole class perform this as a group.

- **SHORT BREAK FOR 15 MINS –**

9. **Reiki Meditation** – Explain this to students and have them perform the technique as a group, with each student focusing on a specific goal to manifest. You may also create a goal for the whole group yourself,

such as each student *"fulfilling their full Reiki potential."*

10. **The Antahkarana** – Show students the four different Tibetan Healing Symbols, explain the differences of each one and how they can be used in treatments and meditations.
11. **Reiki Grid** – Explain how to select crystals, cleanse and charge them and how to set up a Reiki Crystal Grid and charge it daily, either hands on or by using distance Reiki, to empower it from a distance.

- GO FOR LUNCH –

Afternoon Schedule:

1. **Psychic Surgery** – Explain the Psychic Surgery technique and demonstrate this on a student. Then pair up each of your students and have them perform, and receive, Psychic Surgery on one another.
2. **Hui Yin** – Explain how to contract your Hui Yin point to students. Remember that female students have an extra Hui Yin point to contract in their vagina as well as their perineum.
3. **Reiki Master Meditation** – Explain and have students perform the Reiki Master Meditation.
4. **Guided Meditation** – If you wish, you can perform a guided meditation to help empower your students. *See resource section for example.*

REIKI MASTER-TEACHER CLASSES
Taught in a one day class *(usually taught over two days)*

Although there is not a great deal of content to learn in the Reiki Master-Teacher class, the steps involved for performing each of the attunements and techniques are lengthy. As such, it can take some time to memorize each attunement process and technique. One tip to help your students absorb this information as quickly as possible is to prepare a board, or give them a sheet of paper, that explains each part of the attunements using visual imagery. Many people often learn quicker if they have a visual reference of the steps to follow and can look at this while practising each attunement. How you teach is as important as what you teach if you are offering the Master-Teacher course in a one day class.

Suggested class time: 9am - 4pm **or** 10am – 5pm
Morning Session:

1. **Agenda For The Day** – Discuss with your students what the agenda for the day is, mentioning all the points listed in the morning and afternoon class.
2. **Students Talk** – To help break the ice and create group bonding, ask your students to mention why they are doing Reiki & what they hope to achieve from it.
3. **Gift Of The Two Tibetan Master Symbols** – Draw the Tibetan Dai Ko Mio and Fire Serpent and have your students practise drawing them until memorized.
4. **Explanation Of The Tibetan Master Symbols** – Read from the manual the nature of these two Master-Teacher symbols and what each can be used for.
5. **How Attunements Work** – This should be brief as your students should be well versed in the attunement process by this stage.
6. **21-Day-Cleansing Process** – Briefly tell your students what they can expect after the Master-Teacher Attunement.

7. **Give Master-Teacher Attunement** – Give the Master-Teacher Attunement to each of your students.
8. **Reiju Empowerment** – Perform this technique on your students so each can see the process, then have them practise on each other, so both give a Reiju Empowerment and also receive a Reiju empowerment.

– SHORT BREAK FOR 15 MINS -

1. **Healing Attunement** – Perform this technique on your students so each can see the process. Then have them practise on each other, so both give and receive a Healing Attunement.
2. **Reiki Level 1 Attunement** – Perform this technique on your students so each can see the process. Then have them practise on each other, so both give and receive a first degree Reiki attunement.

- GO FOR LUNCH –

Afternoon Schedule:

3. **Reiki Level 2, Reiki Master and Teacher Attunements** - Perform these attunements on your students so each can see the process. Then have them practise each attunement on each other, so all students give and receive each of the Attunement levels. This will easily take up the rest of the afternoon due to the detailed process involved in passing each Attunement.

PART 6:
RESOURCES AND
FORM EXAMPLES

"When one door closes, another opens; but we often look so long and so regretfully upon the closed door that we do not see the one that has opened for us." - **Alexander Graham Bell**

CHAPTER 52
THE LAW AND LEGALITIES

❝ *If you truly loved yourself, you could never hurt another.* ❞
– Buddha

After you have successfully been attuned to Second Degree Usui Reiki and have fulfilled some additional requirements, you are able to get insurance and offer your services to the general public. One thing **ALL** professional Reiki Practitioners should have, if providing Reiki services to the public, is Public Indemnity Insurance, should there be any unforeseen mishaps before, during, or after giving a Reiki treatment. You can find more information and apply for insurance through Balens.co.uk on the UK Reiki Federation website:

- www.Reikifed.co.uk/about-us/31-membership-benefits/55-practitioner-insurance

There has never been any lawsuits won against those who practise Reiki, as working with the Reiki energy is always safe and intelligently guided by spirit. However, there are more down to Earth issues that one should be aware of. For example, if your client fell off your therapy bed, or tripped on your premises before or after their treatment and hurt themselves, you would be open to legal proceedings.

Additionally, **ALL** Reiki practitioners should **ALWAYS** have **EVERY** client complete a disclaimer form prior to receiving their treatment. This ensures you have written evidence of your client agreeing to receive Reiki and helps you keep track of each clients on-going treatments and results. If you do not have clients complete a legal disclaimer form and you are taken to court and successfully sued, your insurance cover *may* be invalidated, leaving you to pay any damages out of your own pocket. You will find disclaimer example forms in this manual or alternatively, you can create your own.

Also be aware that if you are giving Reiki to someone's pet, and that could be anything from a cat or horse to a snake or fish, **ALWAYS** have the pets owner complete a Reiki disclaimer form on behalf of that animal. If you give Reiki to an animal that has not been referred to a vet, or the owner has not signed a disclaimer, you are open to legal proceedings being taken against you and your insurance cover may be invalidated. You will also need to check that your insurance covers you for offering Reiki to animals.

As a final word of caution, if you are ever giving Reiki to children, **ALWAYS** have their parent or guardian complete a disclaimer form on behalf on that child, for similar purposes as listed above, and ask for that child's permission to receive Reiki. Additionally, **ALWAYS INSIST** that the child's parent or guardian sits quietly in the same room as you both and observes the treatment you give to that child. This protects the practitioner from any possible misunderstandings between the Reiki practitioner and the child in question and helps to ensure both child and parent/guardian are relaxed and comfortable with the Reiki treatment being given.

Also ensure you explain the entire procedure and hand positions used during a treatment to **EVERY** client, explaining where your hands will be touching. This avoids any confusion between you and your clients and helps them remain relaxed and comfortable because they know what to expect from their Reiki session.

CHAPTER 53
CLIENT INFORMATION FORMS

❝ Just as a candle can not burn without fire, men can not live without a spiritual life. ❞
– Buddha

The forms you use in your Reiki practice are important. Firstly, they protect you legally. Secondly, they give you a record of each client treatment, what you experienced and what the results of that treatment were. This can be useful in the future and provides a more personalized service to your clients. Thirdly, if you want to join a professional Reiki Regulatory Body, they will want to see detailed records of the treatments you have performed so far. Include the following information in your forms:

Reiki Client Information Form

- Client name
- Address
- Date of Birth
- Phone number, mobile number & e-mail
- Emergency contact details for a relative if desired.
- General Medical Practitioner Contact details

Reiki Client Treatment Form

- Document if client is under the care of a physician
- If they have a medical condition for which a professional diagnosis has been given
- If they are currently receiving medication
- If they have a particular physical, emotional or mental area of concern they wish to work on in this Reiki session
- If they want to stay seated or lie down on a therapy bed during their treatment

- If your client is comfortable with your hands being placed upon their body or prefer not to be touched
- If they are comfortable with you touching their feet
- A short disclaimer *(client consent)*
- The date and both your names and signatures.

A Client Consent example is as follows:

Client Consent

I understand that Reiki is a non-invasive holistic therapy that is used to restore balance in the mind, body and spirit. I understand that Reiki practitioners DO NOT diagnose conditions nor do they prescribe or perform medical treatment, prescribe substances, nor interfere with the treatment of a licensed medical professional. I have been advised that, if I suspect I may have a medical condition, I should seek help from a qualified medical practitioner and that Reiki is not a substitute for professional medical care.

I understand that Reiki can complement any medical or psychological care I may be receiving and that Reiki has the ability to assist the body in healing itself however, I acknowledge that long term imbalances in the body may sometimes require multiple sessions in order to facilitate the level of relaxation needed by the body to heal itself. I confirm that I am 16 years of age or older and that the information I have given is true, to the best of my knowledge, and that I have not withheld any relevant information.

Further to this, I confirm that if any of my given personal information changes, I accept that I must inform the practitioner accordingly upon my next treatment. The practitioner has fully explained the treatment and the procedures involved and I understand that at all times my personal body privacy will be maintained and I am not required to remove any clothing, except my coat and shoes. I confirm that I have had the opportunity to ask questions regarding the above and am willing to proceed with the treatment. I understand that the fee per session is... *(enter the appropriate fee you are charging per session).*

Reiki Client Feedback Form

Document clients name, date of treatment, treatment number, details and duration of Reiki treatment given, client feedback, practitioners notes, aftercare advice and recommended future treatments.

Reiki Client Post-Treatment Information

- This should contain useful information on client aftercare following a treatment. Such as the following:

Reiki Client Post Treatment Information
Practitioner Name:

Aftercare Treatment Advice

Why It's Important To Follow The Aftercare Treatment Advice
Please read the following post Reiki treatment information for details on what to expect following your treatment, what you can do to help promote a naturally healthy balance within your mind, body and spirit and for important facts you should be aware of.

What to expect following your Reiki treatment - Reiki is used holistically, which means it may have a healing effect upon your body and in addition, you may also notice changes in your emotional, psychological and spiritual well-being. You may notice a shift in your consciousness or experience a new level of awareness, in addition to the physical improvements you may notice.

The healing results of Reiki can not always be controlled by a practitioner and directed to a particular physical, emotional, mental or spiritual issue that the client may have. The practitioner only acts as a channel for the Reiki energy to enter into your body where it will always act for your highest and greatest good. As such, it is impossible to determine exactly what clients may experience as every individual will have varying issues that require healing. You should however still notice the benefits of Reiki working on you at any level, whether physical, emotional, mental or spiritual. Following a treatment, it is common for clients to generally feel calm, relaxed and peaceful. On the contrary, some individuals may feel energetic and full of energy following their treatment. Some clients may also experience short-term headaches, feeling emotional, having to urinate more often, discomfort in their stomach, a temporary increase in some symptoms they may be experiencing, needing to sleep or rest more often than usual and in very rare circumstances, may experience temporary physical symptoms, such as a cold or flu like symptoms. These symptoms are a normal part of your bodies healing process and are a sign that energy blockages and negativity in the body are being cleansed and released by the power of Reiki. It is also completely normal not to experience any of the previously mentioned symptoms.

If you have any concerns, please do not hesitate to call your Reiki practitioner or alternatively, contact your doctor should you feel it necessary.

Relax - It is a good idea to try and relax as much as possible for the next three days if you are able to. You may notice yourself being slightly more tired than usual. It is also a good idea to try and avoid any strenuous physical activity for the next few days.

Drink plenty water - Over the next three days especially, it is recommended that you drink plenty of water and keep yourself well hydrated. Reiki will help to release toxins, impurities and negativity from within your body and drinking plenty of water will ensure these are all effectively passed out of your body.

Maintain a healthy diet - It is also a good idea to try and eat healthy foods over the next few days especially, including sufficient amounts of fruits and vegetables. It can also be advantageous to avoid eating meat for the first three days following a Reiki treatment. Also, try to avoid drinking alcohol and consuming caffeine, as this will help to ensure you receive the maximum benefit from your Reiki treatment.

Existing medical conditions - As discussed before your treatment, it will be necessary to monitor your condition if you have conditions such as diabetes, high blood pressure or thyroid problems. After receiving a Reiki treatment, Reiki may help to bring your body into better balance and as a result, the level of medication you are currently receiving may need to be reassessed. If you have any other medical conditions it is a good idea to inform your doctor that you are also receiving a form of holistic energy healing to complement any existing treatment or medication you may be currently on. Everything in the universe is made up of vibrating particles, at the atomic level, and Reiki is also a form of vibratory energy. The body of a qualified, well balanced and healthy Reiki practitioner vibrates at a slightly higher level than non-Reiki practitioners. When you are connected to the healing energy of Reiki, the vibration of your body increases, which causes low vibration negative energies and blockages to release from the body. As a result of a Reiki treatment, toxins and impurities that are stored in your body are released into the blood stream and travel to the kidneys and liver. Your kidneys and liver then filter these toxins and impurities and remove them from your body. As a result of this, an individual may feel some temporary uncomfortable sensations within their body, as already mentioned. Drinking plenty of water will help to flush out the toxins and impurities in your system and minimize any possible discomfort you may feel.

Warning - You should always consult your doctor before changing your diet or increasing your water intake, encase these may affect any conditions, treatments or medication you may be currently receiving.

Reiki Client Treatment Form *(for under 16's)* For clients under 16 years of age, use the same Client Information Form and change the Client Consent accordingly. For example:

267

Client Consent (under 16 year olds)

I understand that Reiki is a non-invasive holistic therapy that is used to restore balance in the mind, body and spirit. I understand that Reiki practitioners DO NOT diagnose conditions nor do they prescribe or perform medical treatment, prescribe substances, nor interfere with the treatment of a licensed medical professional. I have been advised that, I should consult a qualified medical practitioner concerning the health of my child and that Reiki is not a substitute for professional medical care.

I understand that Reiki can complement any medical or psychological care my child may be receiving and that Reiki has the ability to assist the body in healing itself however, I acknowledge that long term imbalances in the body may sometimes require multiple sessions in order to facilitate the level of relaxation needed by the body to heal itself.

I confirm that the information I have given is true, to the best of my knowledge, and that I have not withheld any relevant information. Further to this, I confirm that if any of my child's personal information changes, I accept that I must inform the practitioner accordingly upon my child's next treatment. The practitioner has fully explained the treatment and the procedures involved and I understand that at all times personal body privacy will be maintained and my child is not required to remove any clothing, except their coat and shoes. I confirm that I have had the opportunity to ask questions regarding the above and am willing to proceed with the treatment. As the parent/guardian of _____ I am required to be present during their treatment. I understand that the fee per session is *(enter as appropriate)*.

You can design and print professional looking forms of your own for free, at the '*www.jotform.com*' website.

CHAPTER 54
GUIDED MEDITATION

❝ *In the sky, there is no distinction of East and West; people create distinctions out of their own minds and then believe them to be true.* ❞ **– Buddha**

Perform relaxation technique – Ask students to take a few slow deep breaths, then talk them through relaxing their muscles for a couple minutes. Start with the head and brow, then work down their facial muscles and neck to their shoulders. Slowly and softly telling them that their muscles begin to feel heavy and they feel deeply relaxed. Proceed down their back and arms to the ends of their fingers, down their front to their hips, and flowing down the tops of their legs, calfs and feet, all the way to their toes. Remember to speak slowly, calmly and peacefully and tell your students that they feel deeply relaxed and peaceful on multiple occasions as you guide their relaxation from head to toe. Once your client is deeply relaxed you can proceed.

Now perform the guided meditation – Speak slowly, peacefully and clearly.

1. In front of you is a wide staircase made of clear quartz crystal.

2. Walk over to this staircase until you are standing in front of it.

3. As I count from 1 to 10, begin to climb the stairs, one step at a time, until you reach the landing at the top of the stairs.

4. 1 and 2 and 3 and 4 and 5 and 6 and 7 and 8 and 9 and 10.

5. You are now standing on the landing at the top of the stairs. In front of you is a white door.

6. Slowly walk over to the door and open it. As you open it, you see a white mist in the door frame. Walk through this mist.

7. Remember as you do so that you are safe and protected at all times and are surrounded by Divine light.

8. Before you is a beautiful scene of tall mountains, with a peaceful valley, full of lush green trees and fragrant, colourful flowers in bloom in all shapes and sizes at the bottom.

9. You can smell their floral aroma all around you and feel the gentle breeze blowing your hair.

10. In front of you is a slide, situated in front of a large pool filled with rainbow coloured water

11. Walk over to the slide…and as I count from 1 to 7, climb the stairs of the slide, one step at a time – 1 and 2 and 3 and 4 and 5 and 6 and 7.

12. Sit down on the slide…you are fully dressed, but you don't mind getting wet, as you feel a sense of complete freedom. When you are ready, just slide down into the water below with a smile upon your face.

13. As you gently enter the water, you feel completely at peace and relaxed. You can feel its invigorating, refreshing, crisp, coolness and hear the water as it gently laps against your body and skin.

14. As you float and relax in this rainbow water, be aware of what healing colour your body naturally absorbs.

15. Above you is the yellow glow of the afternoon sun, sharing its loving warmth over your face.

16. You feel so very relaxed, so peaceful, so very happy and filled with warmth, and love.

17. Stay in the water, splash around, and enjoy yourself. And be aware of what else you can see, hear, smell and feel.

Pause for a while or so and let your students experience what is around them. If using this guided meditation during student attunements, perform the attunement at this point. Once finished, continue with the guided meditation to its end.

18. Feel and know, that you are a very loving and powerful channel for the healing energy of Reiki.

19. Feel and know, that you are a powerful healing facilitator who will only perform Reiki for the highest good for self and others.

20. Know that your spirit healing guides will assist you whenever you call upon their help and guidance with a pure, clear and loving heart.

21. Now I am going to count from 1 to 10 and when I reach number 10, you will return to the present time, take 3 slow deep breaths, and open your eyes feeling very refreshed and invigorated.

22. 1...start to come back.....2.....you are slowing returning to conscious awareness.....3....4....you are almost back......5....6.....feel yourself wiggle your toes and move your fingers...7 .....8.....you can feel your whole body coming back to awareness.....9.....10.....you are fully back in the present time.......take 3 slow deep breaths.....feel the loving warmth of Reiki fill your lungs as you inhale and radiate throughout your body.....and when you feel ready, open your eyes.

Mention to your students that if they feel unsteady or dizzy to stay seated, take 3-deep breaths, drink some water and touch an inanimate object to help ground themselves.

This guided meditation can be used during your Reiki Attunements when attuning one person at a time. The pause after the first part of this guided meditation is the point you prepare yourself to give a Reiki Attunement and perform the Reiki Attunement itself.

Ensure your client is deeply relaxed during their attunement, because they will be more receptive to the energy flowing into them and to any messages that may come during the attunement. However performing a guided meditation during an attunement is not necessary.

If you have 3 or more students in your class, it may not be realistic to perform a guided meditation while giving each attunement. Therefore performing it at the end of your class to the whole group is more practical, as the entire guided meditation and attunement can take around 20 minutes. In any case, passing an attunement while performing the guided meditation is not necessary, all that is required is the attunement itself. One would be encouraged to follow their own inner guidance when deciding whether or not to perform a guided meditation for their students.

USEFUL INFORMATION

"Hatred does not cease by hatred, but only by love; this is the eternal rule." **– Buddha**

CHAPTER 55
RECOMMENDED FURTHER READING/WEBSITES

Reiki for Life – by Penelope Quest
Shamanic Reiki – by Llyn Roberts & Robert Levy
Essential Reiki, A Complete Guide To The Ancient Healing Art – by Diane Stein
The Original Reiki Handbook of Dr. Mikao Usui – Dr. Usui, Frank Arjava Petter
The Complete Reiki Handbook – Walter Lubeck
Reiki for the New Millenium – William Lee Rand
Empowerment Through Reiki – Paula Horan
Abundance Through Reiki – Paula Horan
Practical Reiki – Mari Hall
Practising Reiki – Jennie Austin
The Spirit of Reiki – W. Lubeck, Frank Petter, William Rand
A New Earth: Awakening to Your Life's Purpose - E. Tolle
The Mind and Body Bible – Dr. Mark Atkinson
Energy Medicine – Balancing Your Body's Energy for Optimal Health, Joy and Vitality – Donna Eden
Quantum Healing – Deepak Chopra
The Real You Beyond Forms and Lives – Irmansyah Effendi
Revolution X Nefilibata – Ricky Mathieson *(Due out in 2015)*

WEBSITES

www.reiki.org – Hundreds of FREE articles and stories from other Reiki Practitioners. Website of William Lee Rand.
www.reiki.net.au – Scientific studies with Reiki and loads of Reiki/energy related articles.
www.whatthebleep.com – Where Science, Quantum Physics and Spirituality converge.
www.thesecret.com – The Universal Law of Attraction.
www.selfhelphealing.co.uk – 100's of FREE Ebooks and articles relating to various healing practices, self help advice, Reiki training & more. Website of Ricky Mathieson.
www.reikitummo.com – Reiki for safe and instant Kundalini awakening.

REIKI ORGANISATIONS

For information about Reiki training or to contact the author please visit www.selfhelphealing.co.uk. You can also e-mail at: help@selfhelphealing.co.uk

For further information on Reiki Practitioners, Masters and Teachers in your local area, you may find the following organisations and websites useful:

In The UK
UK Reiki Federation – www.reikifed.co.uk
The Reiki Alliance – www.reikialliance.org.uk
The Reiki Association – www.reikiassociation.org.uk
The Reiki Council – www.reikicouncil.org.uk
The General Regulatory Council for Complementary Therapies – www.grcct.org
National Federation of Spiritual Healers – www.nfsh.org.uk
British Complementary Medicine Association – www.bcma.co.uk

In The US & CANADA
The Reiki Alliance – www.reikialliance.com
The International Center for Reiki Training – www.reiki.org
Usui Shiki Ryoho – www.usuireiki-ogm.com
Canadian Reiki Association – www.reiki.ca
Usui-Do – www.usui-do.org
International Association of Reiki Professionals – www.iarp.org

WORLDWIDE
Reiki Dharma – www.reikidharma.com
Reiki Association of South Africa – www.reikihealing.co.za
Reiki Association Southern Africa -www.reikiassociation.co.za
Reiki New Zealand – www.reiki.org.nz
International House of Reiki – www.reiki.net.au

CHAPTER 56
ANCIENT STORIES OF WISDOM - SHINE YOUR LIGHT

"Praise and blame, gain and loss, pleasure and sorrow come and go like the wind. To be happy, rest like a giant tree in the midst of them all." **– Buddha**

We are all born into a dark world and we all need a guiding light to chase away that darkness. In Buddhism, the dark world is comparable to ignorance. The light which chases away the darkness is the light of wisdom. The story of *'The Man and the Small Candle'* can show us an important truth.

66 There was once a small candle carried by a man who was climbing the stairs of a lighthouse. On their way up to the top, the candle asked the man, *"Where are we going?" "We're going to the top of this lighthouse to give signals to the ships upon the ocean,"* the man answered. *"What? How is it possible for me with my small light to give signals to those big ships?",* said the candle weakly, *"They will not be able to see my light". "That's your role. If your light is small, so be it. All you have to do is keep burning and leave the rest to me",* said the man.

A little later, they arrived at the top of the lighthouse where there was a big lamp with a reflector behind it. Then the man lit the lamp with the flame of the candle and instantly, the place shone so brightly that the ships on the ocean could see its light. At this point, the little candle could understand why the man had said to him to *'Keep burning'.* 99

The moral of this story: Even with what we may take to be small ability with limitations, one thing we should bear in mind is that we all have the potential to illuminate the world and each other. All our abilities and expertise will remain as a small light if we show fear and are dismayed when we face the obstacles before us. Through connecting ourselves to the creative-source, we allow our light to amplify and shine far brighter. By becoming one with this powerful energy all around us, we can shine a powerful Divine light that has the power to overcome any obstacles set before us. By connecting our small light to the infinite power of the source, we can tap into a Divine energy that has the power to change the world for the better.

The Buddha said, *"No light is comparable to the light of wisdom"*. The light of wisdom awaits those who learn to tame their wild mind and earthly desires and with the wisdom and power this brings, absolute truth and love shines everywhere without discrimination. As long as your small light keeps burning, you have the power to change not only your own life, but that of everyone else and the world itself.

BE PRESENT IN THE HERE AND NOW

66 A young but earnest Zen student approached his teacher, and asked the Zen Master:

"If I work very hard and diligent how long will it take for me to find Zen."
The Master thought about this, then replied, *"Ten years."*
The student then said, *"But what if I work very hard and really apply myself to learn fast -- How long then ?"*
"Well, twenty years," replied the Master.
"But, if I really work at it and dedicate my life to it. How long then?" asked the student.
"Thirty years," replied the Master.
"But, I do not understand," said the confused student. *"Each time that I say I will work harder, you say it will take me longer. Why is this so?"*
To which the Master replied," *When you have one eye on the goal, you only have one eye on the path."* 99

The moral of this story: Surrendering ourselves to the Divine Source and being in the present moment opens us up to a greater awareness of our capabilities to positively alter our past and future. Really there is no past and there is no future. The past is but a memory and the future an illusion. The only time you will physically exist is in the present moment. When our thoughts and energies are focused upon the past, or distracted by the future, we are no longer living in the present moment. We have no power in the past and we have no power in the future. All of our power exists only in the present moment. We should all see our spiritual path in life as a journey, not a destination. Therefore the goal for each of us should not be to arrive at a certain point in the future. It should be to awaken to a new state of being in the present time. Learn to empty your mind of all thoughts and beliefs and be present in the current moment. When we choose to allow ourselves to become an empty vessel, we prepare our mind and body to receive the enrrgy of love which is necessary for us to achieve enlightenment.

Becoming an empty vessel involves stripping yourself of *everything*. All egos, your beliefs, pre-conceived thoughts, psychological conditioning and the expectations you have placed upon yourself and others. It is becoming at peace with yourself and your surroundings because when we achieve this state of being, we prepare ourselves to receive the full guidance of the Divine Source.

EMPTY YOUR CUP

66 Nan-in, a Japanese master during the Meiji era, received a university professor who came to inquire about achieving enlightenment through spiritual practise.

Nan-in served him tea. He poured his visitor's cup full and continued to keep on pouring.

The professor watched the cup overflow until he could no longer restrain himself. *"The cup is overfull. No more will go in!"*

"Like this cup," Nan-in said, *"you are full of your own opinions*

and speculations. To reach enlightenment, you must first empty your own cup of pre-conceptions?" 🙶

The moral of this story: We have all filled our cups *(our minds)* with preconceptions, beliefs, egos, expectations, prejudices, assumptions, and opinions. We think we already know what we are and need, or where to find out what we are or need. But the spiritual path to enlightenment requires that we disregard what we think we know. Rather, we must open our consciousness and trust that what we need will be given to us from the creative-source. We must be willing to let go of our past mental constructs and be open and willing to change our minds to accept truth.

A truly opened mind is a mind that is free from all thinking and belief and as already mentioned, when we allow ourselves to become an empty vessel, we prepare ourselves to receive enlightenment. If we do not first empty ourselves, our primitive human brain will only serve to hamper our journey while on our spiritual path. Your lives purpose is less to do with creating your destiny yourself. It's more to do with being aware of its unfolding before your eyes.

CHAPTER 57
FINAL THOUGHTS - YOUR JOURNEY HAS JUST STARTED

66 *There are only two mistakes one can make along the road to truth; not going all the way, and not starting.* 99 - **Buddha**

Never be stagnant...

Whether you have only recently entered the world of Reiki or have ventured further and become a Reiki Master-Teacher, you should be grateful and content for the direction you have found. However, being content should not cause you to become stagnant. Being a Reiki Master-Teacher doesn't mean you have found your destination. It only means you have started upon a lifetime path towards enlightenment.

No matter if you are a Reiki Master, a Spiritual Guru or the Dalai Lama himself, if you still exist on this physical plane you still have something to learn. We never stop learning just as much as we never stop experiencing and for the Reiki practitioner that understands this and strives to become better, more aware and more refined, the more they will provide for both themselves and for others.

Usui Reiki is just the first step in a long journey and you may well find that journey involves learning other disciplines which you never expected to venture into. Reiki will guide you to where you need to be if you ask for that guidance, surrender to the Divine source and be completely open to change and progress. Surrendering and being open does not mean you become submissive. It simply means you realize where your real power truly lies. Put your faith and trust in this Divine guidance and you will experience and enjoy life on a far higher level. Remember the power of your intentions. If you want something, ask for it and the more specific your intentions are, the more specific the response.

Helping others to help yourself…

Helping yourself first and foremost is important and all Reiki practitioners would be encouraged to work on balancing themselves physically, emotionally, mentally and spiritually and continuing to do so for the rest of their lives. When we are personally in a state of balance and harmony within ourselves, we are better prepared to help create this same equilibrium within others. However this doesn't mean you shouldn't share the gift of Reiki with others or not give treatments. By using and developing a relationship with the Reiki symbols and energies in any way will only help improve your connection to source and help increase the flow of Reiki being channelled through you. Using Reiki as often as possible, whether on yourself or on others, would be strongly advised. And there is a very good reason for making the time and effort to help those around you.

Humanity is one conscious organism. Every one of us is interconnected by an intelligent energy that flows around us and through us. This is the energy of love in its purest form. As we are all connected, our individual actions cause a reflection upon every other person and the collective consciousness as a whole. So what changes in one individual naturally ripples down this web of energy to everyone and everything else. *'Love others unconditionally and unconditional love will be returned to you'*. This is one of the Universal laws.

Like attracts like in the unseen world. Match your own energy with that which you desire and you shall receive it. When you project love and compassion from a pure and genuine heart, you choose to resonate yourself with the energies of love and compassion. These same energies are then returned to you.

If you are to live a happy and joyful life today, you must be able to let go of yesterday. Otherwise your thoughts become mechanical in your day to day life. A mechanical mind can not discover what True Love is or become aware of your true nature as to not *who* you are, but *what* you are. We are all genetically programmed to seek love for ourselves, however many individuals make the common mistake of seeking that love from another individual in order to fill that void inside our hearts. The reason the vast majority of relationships break down is because many of us are looking for the wrong type of love and we are looking for it in all the wrong places.

True Love, that spark of Divine energy that can be channelled through our hearts and bodies, is a selfless love. It is a love without competition and jealousy, without conditions and a desire to control and possess another individual because one has become dependent on the emotional security their intimate relationships bring them. True Love, which many are unknowingly seeking, will never be found from another individual or by knowledge and intellect alone. It can only be realized through the proper use of your heart.

When you abandon your beliefs, your egos and you discard everything you have come to learn about *who* you think you are and what you think love truly is, you lay the necessary foundation for awakening to your true nature. The spiritual path forward needs no thought. It only requires that you learn to open your heart.

In order to open your heart, you must be willing and able to let go of everything that does not serve your higher purpose. Your attachments to the material world is one necessary evil you should strive to conquer because at the root of all your pain and suffering is attachment. Your attachments are the origin of this pain and suffering. Therefore attachment is the cause of all pain and suffering, whether that's an attachment to a belief, an ideal, a thought, a principle, an expectation, a religion, a lover, ones self-image or anything else within the material world.

When one has an attachment to material things, for example, one should strive to detach from such an unhealthy state of mind. When one sees an object as being attractive, unattractive, or neutral, feelings of pleasure, pain or neutrality invariably arise. It is because of such feelings that attachment develops, whether that's an attachment of not wanting to separate from pleasure or the attachment of wanting to separate from pain.

Every day we see things that bring us pleasure, people we like, foods we enjoy and attractive materials we would like to buy or incorporate into our lives. To fill our lives with the things we superficially love seems natural, but in truth, this mentality is the path that leads to pain and suffering for these things can never be sustained. A mind that is cluttered and clouded by attachment can never be free from its bondage and can never know peace or True Love. Only when one empties oneself of all attachments can peace of mind and True Love be realized.

If one blindly follows the so-called norms of society and conforms to the external conditioning of religion, society and accepted mainstream forms of institutionalized thought, self-realization will never be achieved. Conforming allows for a greater acceptance by our peers, however in the process of conforming, one becomes stagnant, mechanical in their day to day lives and filled with the pains and sufferings of attachment.

You carry all the power needed within yourself to imagine a better world. You *are* humanity. In order for humanity to change, you must first change yourself.

Love and light on your journey.

Namaste -
I honour the light, love, truth, beauty and peace within you because it's also within me. In sharing these things we are united. We are the same. We are one.

Printed in Great Britain
by Amazon